Spiritual Warfare

Lance G Jones

ISBN: 978-1-9993164-6-4

Table of Contents

The Call to Spiritual Warfare

As a new Christian, I was unaware that I had been drafted into a spiritual army. Initially, I believed my journey would be straightforward and free of challenges, not realising there were unseen forces working against me. It took time for me to understand that engaging in spiritual warfare was essential and required my active participation.

I recall moments when spiritual battles became so intense that they impacted my physical life. These relentless attacks tested my endurance, and without clear guidance, I had to learn through personal experiences anchored in the Word of God and empowered by the Holy Spirit. Each trial reinforced that spiritual warfare is not just a concept but a reality that demands vigilance, prayer, and unwavering faith. Most importantly, it requires the assistance of the Holy Spirit.

The intensity of the battle varies for each person, influenced by factors such as one's calling, ministry area, and desire to know God. It is often said that ***"The devil will never trouble those he already has."*** While its absolute truth is debatable, it underscores a reality: those striving to follow God will face resistance.

Spiritual warfare is a crucial aspect of the Christian life, involving an ongoing, unseen battle. Believers are not mere spectators but active participants, called to engage with divine empowerment and wisdom. Forces beyond the visible world influence daily lives, seeking to distract, sway, or oppress. Yet through Christ, we have the authority to stand firm.

The Bible speaks of an unseen realm where spiritual forces operate.

"For we wrestle not against flesh and blood, but against principalities, against powers, against the rulers of the darkness of this world, against spiritual wickedness in high places." **Ephesians 6:12**

Recognising this truth helps believers respond with discernment and strength. Our challenges are not solely physical but have spiritual roots. Understanding this empowers us to act with faith, knowing that every prayer and step of obedience disrupts the enemy's plans and furthers God's purposes.

"For though we walk in the flesh, we do not war after the flesh: For the weapons of our warfare are not carnal, but mighty through God to the pulling down of strongholds." **2 Corinthians 10:3-4**

This reinforces that our strength is not of human origin but comes from God. Our reliance is on His power, not on human strategies.

Our spiritual weapons carry divine power to demolish strongholds, fortified barriers in the mind that resist God's truth. Achieving spiritual victory means depending on God's strength. True power is found in surrendering to His authority and allowing Him to guide us.

When we rely on God as our source, we can face the enemy without fear, knowing His strength is perfected in our weaknesses. This understanding equips us to engage confidently, assured that we do not fight alone but under His protection and guidance with weapons not designed by men.

The Weapons of Our Warfare

Understanding the nature of spiritual warfare is vital, but recognising the divine tools at our disposal is equally important. God equips believers with powerful spiritual weapons to overcome unseen adversaries and stand firm in faith. Without these weapons, believers risk being unprepared for the inevitable battles that come with living a life dedicated to God.

One of the most significant weapons is prayer. Prayer is more than speaking to God; it is direct communication that aligns the heart with His will and invites divine intervention. It is a strategic weapon that not only strengthens the believer but also disrupts the enemy's plans.

"The effectual fervent prayer of a righteous man availeth much." **James 5:16**

Through prayer, believers find strength, guidance, and resilience to face spiritual battles. It is through fervent and persistent prayer that breakthroughs occur, strongholds are broken, and divine power is released.

Prayer is also a means of engaging in intercession—not just for oneself but for others who may be under attack. Later chapters will explore deeper aspects of prayer and intercession, highlighting their transformative power in warfare.

Fasting amplifies prayer's impact, deepening spiritual focus and fostering a greater reliance on God. Fasting is an act of spiritual discipline that subdues the flesh, heightens sensitivity to the Holy Spirit, and demonstrates complete dependence on God. Jesus emphasised its importance when He said:

"Howbeit this kind goeth not out but by prayer and fasting."
Matthew 17:21

Fasting sharpens spiritual awareness, making it an essential practice for overcoming significant spiritual challenges. It is a means of breaking spiritual oppression, gaining divine clarity, and positioning oneself for supernatural breakthroughs. Many biblical figures, including Moses, Daniel, and Esther, incorporated fasting into their spiritual battles, demonstrating its power in shifting spiritual realities.

Genuine worship is another powerful weapon. Worship shifts the focus from problems to God's power, inviting His presence into our struggles and disrupting the enemy's plans. True worship is not merely about singing songs; it is a heart posture that acknowledges God's sovereignty and welcomes His intervention. When believers worship in spirit and truth, they create an atmosphere where God's presence dwells and the enemy is silenced.

The Word of God is a powerful tool at our disposal, which we will look at in later chapters.

The name of Jesus carries unparalleled authority. His name is not just a title but a declaration of power and dominion.

"That at the name of Jesus, every knee should bow, of things in heaven, and things in earth, and things under the earth." **Philippians 2:10**

Invoking His name in faith brings divine power to confront spiritual challenges. Demons tremble at the mention of His name, and strongholds are broken when believers stand in the authority that Jesus has given them. Understanding the power of His name equips believers to walk in boldness, knowing that they operate under divine authority.

Faith acts as a shield, as described in **Ephesians 6:16**:

"Above all, taking the shield of faith, wherewith ye shall be able to quench all the fiery darts of the wicked."

Faith is more than belief; it is absolute trust in God's promises. It is a defensive and offensive weapon that neutralises the enemy's attacks and enables believers to persevere. Trusting in God's promises enables believers to resist attacks and remain steadfast, turning doubt into assurance. A faith-filled believer cannot be easily shaken because their confidence is anchored in God's unchanging nature.

Obedience to God's Word is another vital weapon. Many people desire victory in spiritual warfare but struggle because they are not fully submitted to God's authority. The Bible reminds us:

"Behold, to obey is better than sacrifice." **1 Samuel 15:22**

Obedience aligns believers with God's will and strengthens their spiritual position. The enemy thrives on disobedience and rebellion, but those who walk in obedience shut the door to demonic influence and walk in divine protection. When we submit to God and resist the devil, the enemy has no choice but to flee.

Another overlooked but powerful weapon is the blood of Jesus. The blood of Christ is a declaration of victory over sin, death, and the works of the enemy.

"And they overcame him by the blood of the Lamb, and by the word of their testimony." **Revelation 12:11**

The blood of Jesus is a seal of divine protection and a reminder that the enemy has already been defeated. Pleading the blood of Jesus over one's life, family, and circumstances is a powerful declaration that no weapon formed against the believer shall prosper.

These weapons, empowered by the Holy Spirit, equip believers to stand against the enemy confidently. When used collectively—The name of Jesus, prayer, fasting, worship, Scripture, faith, obedience, and the blood of Jesus—they form a comprehensive defence and offence, ensuring victory in spiritual battles.

Recognising and employing these weapons empowers believers to navigate spiritual challenges effectively and securely in the knowledge that God's strength is their foundation. No matter how intense the battle, victory is guaranteed for those who stand firm in Christ, wielding the weapons He has provided.

In the next chapter, we will explore how the name of Jesus and the blood of Jesus play pivotal roles in spiritual warfare, highlighting their spiritual significance and impact.

The Name of Jesus and the Blood

In generations past, Christians frequently used the terms **"pleading the blood of Jesus"** and **"In the name of Jesus"** as powerful declarations of faith in spiritual warfare. These phrases were not mere traditions but expressions of deep understanding of the authority given to believers. When faced with danger, oppression, or demonic attacks, early believers would boldly **plead the blood of Jesus** as a spiritual covering, recalling the power of Christ's sacrifice. Likewise, **calling on the name of Jesus** was a battle cry, an unshakable declaration that invoked the authority of the risen Christ. Scripture affirms this power:

"And they overcame him by the blood of the Lamb," **Revelation 12:11a.**

This truth remains unchanged—just as the early Church cast out devils and performed miracles in Jesus' name, believers today have access to the same supernatural authority.

Yet, modern-day Christianity seems to have lost much of this fervour. In an age where many prioritise intellectual reasoning and self-reliance over spiritual authority, these once-powerful declarations are now rarely heard. Many have exchanged the supernatural aspects of faith for a more passive or intellectual approach, forgetting that true victory comes through the **blood and the name of Jesus**. Yet, the potency of these spiritual weapons has not diminished. The Word remains clear:

"Wherefore God also hath highly exalted him, and given him a name which is above every name: That at the name of Jesus every knee should bow, of things in heaven, and things in earth, and things under the earth." **Philippians 2:9-10**.

The blood of Jesus still speaks on behalf of believers today, just as it did in the days of old:

"And to Jesus the mediator of the new covenant, and to the blood of sprinkling, that speaketh better things than that of Abel." **Hebrews 12:24**.

It is time for the Church to reclaim these truths, standing once more in the authority that has never faded.

Understanding the power of the blood of Jesus and the name of Jesus is fundamental for believers navigating spiritual warfare. These divine tools are not just symbols of faith but profound sources of spiritual strength and victory. Before exploring expressions such as praise, clapping and shouting as acts of spiritual engagement in the next chapters, it is essential to grasp the significance of these powerful elements that fortify a believer's foundation.

The Blood of Jesus: A Shield and a Seal

The blood of Jesus holds unparalleled power in the spiritual realm. It is more than a historical mark of sacrifice; it is an eternal covenant of redemption, protection, and victory. The cleansing power of His blood ensures that believers stand justified before God, free from the condemnation of sin.

In spiritual warfare, the blood of Jesus acts as both a shield and a seal. This victory over spiritual adversaries is achieved through the declaration and application of Jesus' sacrificial blood.

"And they overcame him by the blood of the Lamb, and by the word of their testimony; and they loved not their lives unto the death." **Revelation 12:11**

Believers can invoke this power as a protective covering, ensuring that they are safeguarded from the attacks of the enemy. Through faith and proclamation, the blood of Jesus provides an unassailable defence and assurance of triumph over all spiritual forces.

The blood of Jesus also signifies the ultimate defeat of Satan. At the cross, Jesus disarmed principalities and powers, triumphing over them openly:

Thus, when believers invoke the blood, they are affirming this triumphant truth and standing firm in the victory that Christ secured.

It has been said that **one drop of the blood of Jesus** is more powerful than all the forces of hell combined, and this truth is deeply rooted in Scripture. The blood of Christ was not merely human—it was divine, carrying the very life of God, and it was through this blood that Satan was utterly defeated.

"Neither by the blood of goats and calves, but by his own blood he entered in once into the holy place, having obtained eternal redemption for us." **Hebrews 9:12**.

No demonic power can stand against the blood that was shed on Calvary, for it is the seal of victory, the payment for sin, and the weapon that dismantles every work of darkness.

The enemy trembles at the mention of the blood because it is the evidence of his eternal defeat. No curse, bondage, or attack of the adversary can withstand the authority of Christ's blood, for it still speaks, it still delivers, and it still conquers.

The Name of Jesus: Authority and Power

The name of Jesus is not just a revered title; it is the embodiment of divine authority. The name of Jesus is highly exalted and commands submission from every force, seen and unseen.

This powerful truth is illustrated in the book of Acts, where Paul cast out the spirit of divination from a girl:

"And this did she many days. But Paul, being grieved, turned and said to the spirit, I command thee in the name of Jesus Christ to come out of her. And he came out the same hour." **Acts 16:18**

When believers call on the name of Jesus, they are invoking the authority He holds over all creation. The apostles' accounts in the book of Acts show how they healed the sick, cast out demons, and performed miracles in His name. This underscores that the name of Jesus is a source of salvation and deliverance for all.

In moments of spiritual opposition, calling on the name of Jesus is a declaration of faith that signals to the forces of darkness that they must retreat. The power in His name lies not just in its utterance but in the faith behind it. Believers must understand that when they speak the name of Jesus, they are activating divine intervention and accessing the full authority of heaven.

Many a night, I would wake up to an oppressive, evil presence that filled my room. The fear was tangible, weighing heavily on me, and it felt like darkness had taken hold. In those moments, I found strength in what I knew to be my greatest spiritual defence: the blood of Jesus. Each time, I would plead the blood of Jesus, speaking it aloud with unwavering faith. Immediately, the oppressive atmosphere would lift, and the dark presence would leave my room. The peace that followed was undeniable, a reminder of the power and protection that comes through Jesus' sacrifice.

In addition, I have taken countless numbers of people through deliverance, casting out demons in the name of Jesus. Each time, the spiritual forces that sought to oppress and afflict were driven out, proving that the authority of His name is unmatched and absolute. These experiences have reinforced my faith and shown me time and again that victory is always secured through the mighty name of Jesus.

The Combined Forces of Blood and Name

Together, the blood of Jesus and the name of Jesus create an unyielding defence and powerful offensive strategy in spiritual warfare. By covering oneself with the blood of Jesus and speaking His name, believers reinforce their stance against spiritual threats. It is a practice that aligns them with the victory won at Calvary and the authority granted through Christ's resurrection.

Understanding these truths prepares believers to engage in further expressions of faith, such as clapping and shouting, with the confidence that they are protected and empowered by the most potent spiritual forces available. Equipped with the knowledge of the blood and the name of Jesus, believers can step into any spiritual battle knowing their foundation is strong and their victory assured.

The Word of God

The Word of God is described as *"the sword of the Spirit"* in **Ephesians 6:17**. It is an active weapon used to counter deception and temptation. Jesus wielded the Scriptures effectively against Satan during His temptation:

"It is written, Man shall not live by bread alone, but by every word that proceedeth out of the mouth of God." **Matthew 4:4**

This encounter illustrates that declaring God's truth is essential for victory. The Word of God exposes lies, strengthens faith, and serves as a weapon against every attack of the enemy. By immersing oneself in Scripture, believers arm themselves with divine truth that cuts through spiritual darkness.

"For the word of God is quick, and powerful, and sharper than any twoedged sword, piercing even to the dividing asunder of soul and spirit, and of the joints and marrow, and is a discerner of the thoughts and intents of the heart." **Hebrews 4:12**

A **two-edged** sword cuts both ways, signifying that the Word of God not only defends against attacks but also convicts and transforms the believer. It penetrates deeply, exposing truth and falsehood and bringing both judgment and healing.

This is why believers are called to wield it with wisdom and understanding:

"Study to shew thyself approved unto God, a workman that needeth not to be ashamed, rightly dividing the word of truth." **2 Timothy 2:15**

The Bible reveals that Jesus Himself, in His second coming, will wield the **sharp two-edged sword** to bring judgment and establish His righteousness:

"And out of his mouth goeth a sharp sword, that with it he should smite the nations: and he shall rule them with a rod of iron: and he treadeth the winepress of the fierceness and wrath of Almighty God." **Revelation 19:15**

The **two-edged nature** of God's Word means that it not only **destroys** the works of the enemy but also **purifies and refines** the believer:

"Is not my word like as a fire? saith the LORD; and like a hammer that breaketh the rock in pieces?" **Jeremiah 23:29**

For this reason, believers must not only **hear** the Word but also **apply it:**

"But be ye doers of the word, and not hearers only, deceiving your own selves." **James 1:22**

Through Scripture, believers gain wisdom and discernment, equipping them to resist the enemy's schemes:

"Every word of God is pure: he is a shield unto them that put their trust in him." **Proverbs 30:5**

By declaring and living according to **God's two-edged Sword**, believers walk in authority, discernment, and victory, ensuring that the enemy is defeated and God's kingdom is established.

Praise in Warfare

Praise is a powerful act of spiritual defiance and connection to God. It is essential for strengthening believers during spiritual warfare. While prayer often involves asking for God's intervention, praise focuses on acknowledging and exalting His power, presence, and holiness.

"The Lord reigneth; let the people tremble: he sitteth between the cherubims; let the earth be moved. The Lord is great in Zion; and he is high above all the people. Let them praise thy great and terrible name; for it is holy." **Psalm 99:1-3**

Praise has a twofold effect in spiritual warfare: it serves as both a defence and an offence. It shifts the atmosphere, invites God's presence, and confuses the enemy. It is not merely an act of worship but a weapon that has the power to dismantle the strategies of the adversary. The biblical accounts of Jehoshaphat, Paul and Silas, and others illustrate that praise is more than a religious exercise—it is a battle strategy ordained by God.

1. Praise Confuses and Defeats the Enemy

A profound example of the power of praise is found in **2 Chronicles 20**, where King Jehoshaphat faced a formidable alliance of enemies. In response, Jehoshaphat called for a national fast and sought the Lord's guidance. God reassured him through a prophetic word:

"Be not afraid nor dismayed by reason of this great multitude; for the battle is not yours, but God's." **2 Chronicles 20:15**

Acting on this assurance, Jehoshaphat appointed singers to go ahead of the army, singing:

"Praise the Lord; for his mercy endureth forever." **2 Chronicles 20:21**

As they began to sing and praise, Scripture records:

"The LORD set ambushments against the children of Ammon, Moab, and mount Seir, which were come against Judah; and they were smitten." **2 Chronicles 20:22**

This miraculous victory demonstrates that praise can confuse and defeat the enemy, highlighting God's power through the praise of His people.

There was a day when everything was going wrong. The enemy had orchestrated a series of challenges designed to wear me down, filling my heart with frustration and discouragement. In the past, I might have fallen into the trap of complaining, allowing negativity to take root and giving the devil an open door to further torment my mind. But on this particular day, something rose within me—a determination not to give in to his schemes. Instead of voicing my frustrations, I decided I would praise God.

With tears in my eyes and a heavy heart, I lifted my hands and began to give God praise. I declared God's goodness, His faithfulness, and His power over my situation. I sang songs of victory, thanking Him in advance for the breakthrough, even though my circumstances had not yet changed. As I praised, something incredible happened—the weight of oppression lifted, and a supernatural peace filled my spirit. I realised that my praise had not only strengthened me but had completely disrupted the enemy's plans. He wanted me to sink into despair, but instead, I had given glory to God.

That day, I learned a powerful truth: praise confuses the enemy. He expects us to react in fear, doubt, and frustration when faced with trials, but when we choose to exalt God instead, we deny the devil the outcome he desires. My praise shifted the atmosphere, bringing God's presence into my situation, and soon, the victory I had been seeking was manifested. What the enemy meant for evil, God turned for good, and I walked away not just with a breakthrough but with a deeper revelation of the power of praise in spiritual warfare.

2. Praise Invites the Presence of God

The act of praise creates an environment where God's presence is invited to move powerfully. Praise shifts the believer's focus from fear and uncertainty to faith and confidence in God's sovereignty.

"It came even to pass, as the trumpeters and singers were as one, to make one sound to be heard in praising and thanking the Lord; and when they lifted up their voice with the trumpets and cymbals and instruments of musick, and praised the Lord, saying, For he is good; for his mercy endureth for ever: that then the house was filled with a cloud, even the house of the Lord; So that the priests could not stand to minister by reason of the cloud: for the glory of the Lord had filled the house of God." **2 Chronicles 5:13-14**

This signifies that God dwells within the praise of His people. When believers face challenges and choose to praise, they align themselves with God's will and release His divine intervention into their circumstances.

3. Praise Brings Deliverance

Praise has the power to break chains and set captives free. A striking example is seen in the lives of Paul and Silas:

"And at midnight Paul and Silas prayed, and sang praises unto God: and the prisoners heard them. And suddenly there was a great earthquake, so that the foundations of the prison were shaken: and immediately all the doors were opened, and every one's bands were loosed." **Acts 16:25-26**

Their praise did not just bring personal deliverance but also affected everyone around them. This highlights the ability of praise to release supernatural breakthroughs.

4. Praise Brings Peace and Assurance

Engaging in praise and moving into worship during times of struggle brings peace and assurance.

"Thou wilt keep him in perfect peace, whose mind is stayed on thee: because he trusteth in thee." **Isaiah 26:3**

Praise helps believers shift their focus from the problem to God's sovereignty and might. It is an act of trust that reaffirms God's dominion over all circumstances.

5. Praise Strengthens Faith and Reminds of God's Faithfulness

Praise also serves as a reminder of God's past faithfulness, fuelling the believer's faith for present and future challenges. Remembering His deeds and praising Him for who He is aligns the believer's heart with His will, making them more attuned to His voice and guidance.

6. Praise as a Lifestyle of Warfare

Incorporating praise into daily life goes beyond songs and services; it includes a lifestyle of gratitude, humility, and devotion.

Living in an attitude of praise fortifies the spirit and prepares the believer for spiritual encounters, ensuring they are always battle-ready.

Praise is not merely a response to blessings but a strategic tool in spiritual warfare. It is both a shield and a sword, a defence against fear and an offensive weapon against the enemy's attacks. As seen throughout Scripture, when believers engage in praise, they invite God's presence, confuse the enemy, and position themselves for divine victory. Whether facing personal struggles, spiritual battles, or overwhelming circumstances, let praise be your weapon, for *"the battle is not yours, but God's."* **2 Chronicles 20:15**.

As we have explored the power of praise in Warfare, let us now move on to looking at how clapping and shouting can be effective in our warfare.

Clap Your Hands and Shout

Throughout the Bible, the clapping of hands and shouting are presented as expressions of triumph, joy, and powerful acts of faith that influence the spiritual atmosphere. These physical acts, while simple, carry deep spiritual significance and can be used as effective tools in spiritual warfare.

Clapping hands is often associated with celebration and victory.

"O clap your hands, all ye people; shout unto God with the voice of triumph." **Psalm 47:1**

This verse illustrates that clapping is more than an expression of joy; it is a declaration of victory over the enemy. It signifies confidence in God's power to overcome adversity and disrupt the spiritual forces working against believers. However, clapping is not only used for celebration. In certain contexts, it can signify disdain and the defeat of evil forces.

"Men shall clap their hands at him, and shall hiss him out of his place." **Job 27:23**

This demonstrates that clapping can be an act of spiritual defiance, acknowledging the enemy's downfall and reinforcing God's victory.

Shouting, on the other hand, is often linked to breakthrough and deliverance. The walls of Jericho provide a notable example:

"So the people shouted when the priests blew with the trumpets: and it came to pass, when the people heard the sound of the trumpet, and the people shouted with a great shout, that the wall fell down flat." **Joshua 6:20**

This story emphasises that a shout, rooted in faith and obedience, can trigger divine intervention and dismantle barriers. Shouting can also signify judgment and the release of God's power.

"The LORD shall roar from on high, and utter his voice from his holy habitation; he shall mightily roar upon his habitation; he shall give a shout." **Jeremiah 25:30**

This powerful imagery shows that shouting can symbolise the authority of God being proclaimed, resulting in victory over darkness.

When believers incorporate clapping and shouting into their worship and spiritual warfare, they align their physical actions with expressions of faith that echo biblical truths. These acts are not mere rituals; they are declarations of trust in God's power and a means to shift the spiritual atmosphere.

Often, during worship services, there are moments when I feel an unction to respond in ways that might seem unusual or spontaneous. It could be an overwhelming urge to clap my hands or shout in praise. These acts often arise unexpectedly, but over time, I have learned to recognise them as divine promptings, a call to engage in a deeper way with the atmosphere of worship. When I feel that stirring, I no longer hesitate; I respond in obedience. Clapping or shouting may seem simple, but I have witnessed the power of such actions in shifting the spiritual atmosphere and bringing breakthroughs.

The act of clapping or shouting was not merely a physical expression of joy; it was an act of obedience that invited God's presence in a powerful way. I have seen situations where heavy burdens were lifted, spiritual breakthroughs occurred, and even the oppression of the enemy seemed to break under the force of that simple act. It is as if, in that moment of obedience, heaven responds with divine intervention, dismantling strongholds and clearing paths for breakthroughs.

I have come to realise that these acts of clapping or shouting are not just for moments of joy or celebration, but they are often times of warfare in the spirit. Through them, I align myself with God's will, declaring His victory, His power, and His authority over every situation. When I act in faith, stepping out in obedience to what might seem like a small, simple gesture, I have experienced just how profound the impact of obedience can be, seeing lives transformed and spiritual barriers broken. These moments of unction have become a reminder that God can use even the smallest act of obedience to bring about great change and breakthrough.

Clapping hands and shouting are effective, faith-driven acts that enhance spiritual warfare. They symbolise victory, disrupt the enemy's plans, and invite God's intervention. By embracing these actions, believers can reinforce their spiritual position and celebrate the assured triumph given by God.

In the following chapter, we will explore how your testimony can be a source of strength for the hearer and a powerful tool of deliverance.

The Power of your Testimony

Testimonies are powerful tools in the believer's spiritual arsenal. Sharing personal experiences of God's faithfulness and deliverance serves to strengthen faith, inspire others, and build spiritual resilience. Revelation 12:11 underscores the importance of testimony:

"And they overcame him by the blood of the Lamb, and by the word of their testimony; and they loved not their lives unto the death."

The Role of Testimonies in Warfare

1. Affirming God's Power: Testimonies remind believers of God's omnipotence. When people recount their encounters with God's intervention, it reinforces faith and highlights that His power is ever-present. Such stories disrupt the enemy's narrative of defeat by highlighting victory.
2. Hearing others' stories of overcoming adversity brings hope to those facing similar battles.

3. Testimonies confirm that God is faithful to deliver, inspiring listeners to trust in His promises.

4. Sharing testimonies builds unity and strengthens the bond among believers.

Overcoming Challenges to Sharing Testimonies

The enemy seeks to silence believers through fear, shame, or doubt. Breaking through these barriers requires boldness and reliance on the Holy Spirit. When believers step forward and share their testimonies, they assert their spiritual authority and weaken the enemy's grip.

Using Testimonies in Prayer and Worship

Integrating testimonies into prayer sessions and worship reinforces faith and collective gratitude. Recalling God's past deeds during prayer helps believers maintain hope and expectation for future victories. Worship that includes moments of testimony creates an atmosphere of praise, where God's presence is welcomed, and the enemy is reminded of his defeat.

Testimonies are not just stories; they are declarations of God's continued work in the lives of His people. By embracing and sharing these powerful narratives, believers can maintain a posture of victory and faith, inspiring others and reinforcing their own resolve.

As a preacher, I get to Testify all the time and have encouraged and blessed others with the wonders that the LORD has done in my life.

In the next chapters, we will examine a few more of the spiritual weapons and tools we have at our disposal.

Our testimonies strengthen our faith and reaffirm our authority in Christ. With this foundation, we can now explore the spiritual authority given to us through binding and loosing.

Binding and Loosing

Jesus spoke about binding and loosing in **Matthew 16:19**:

"And I will give unto thee the keys of the kingdom of heaven: and whatsoever thou shalt bind on earth shall be bound in heaven: and whatsoever thou shalt loose on earth shall be loosed in heaven."

This verse highlights the authority believers have to impact the spiritual realm.

The Origin of Binding and Loosing

The terms "binding and loosing" originate from Jewish rabbinic tradition, where they refer to the authority of rabbis to permit or forbid certain actions based on scriptural interpretation. In the biblical context, Jesus used these terms to convey the spiritual authority given to believers, particularly in relation to prayer, spiritual warfare, and establishing God's will on earth.

Understanding Binding

Binding is an act of restricting or limiting spiritual forces that oppose God's will. It involves a proactive declaration to halt demonic interference and activity.

Examples of Binding in Prayer and Their Outcomes

- **Binding Fear and Anxiety:** I bind the spirit of fear and anxiety, for God hath not given me the spirit of fear; but of power, and of love, and of a sound mind (2 Timothy 1:7). **Outcome:** I walk in boldness, love, and a sound mind.
- **Binding Sickness and Disease:** I bind every spirit of infirmity and declare that by His stripes, I am healed (Isaiah 53:5). **Outcome:** I receive divine healing and restoration.
- **Binding Confusion and Deception:** I bind every spirit of confusion and deception, for God is not the author of confusion, but of peace (1 Corinthians 14:33). **Outcome:** I walk in divine clarity and truth.
- **Binding Lack and Poverty:** I bind the spirit of lack and poverty, for my God shall supply all my needs according to His riches in glory by Christ Jesus (Philippians 4:19). **Outcome:** I live in God's provision and abundance.
- **Binding Attacks of the Enemy:** I bind every weapon formed against me, for no weapon that is formed against me shall prosper (Isaiah 54:17). **Outcome:** I walk in divine protection and victory.

When binding, reinforce the action with relevant scriptures to affirm spiritual authority.

Understanding Loosing

Loosing involves releasing or permitting God's power and blessings into a situation, such as peace, joy, healing, or freedom.

Speaking Life Over Situations: Affirm God's promises to invite His presence. For instance, declaring, "I loose peace that surpasses all understanding over my home", helps establish an environment where divine peace dispels fear and anxiety. This practice can be applied to various circumstances—workplaces, family conflicts, or personal struggles—ensuring God's presence and power are active.

Binding secures the battle, but loosing ensures the victory. The true blessing lies in the act of loosing—releasing God's power and purpose so that His Kingdom is realised on Earth as it is in Heaven.

Examples of Loosing in Prayer and Their Outcomes

- **Loosing Spiritual Blessings**: I loose the spirit of wisdom and revelation over my life, as written in Ephesians 1:17. **Outcome:** I walk in divine insight and understanding.

- **Loosing Blessings and Prosperity**: I loose God's favour, abundance, and provision over my finances and projects. **Outcome:** I experience divine breakthroughs and prosperity.
- **Loosing Healing and Restoration**: I loose divine healing and restoration in my body and mind. **Outcome:** I walk in wholeness and renewed strength.
- **Loosing Joy and Strength**: I loose the joy of the Lord, which is my strength, into my life and the lives of my loved ones. **Outcome:** I am filled with joy and empowered to overcome.

Understanding the power of binding and loosing, coupled with the power of declaring, will shift your warfare to the next level.

Now, let us look at a subject that not a lot of people know about or understand in its entirety: Spiritual Mapping.

Spiritual Mapping

Spiritual mapping is a practice within Christian intercessory prayer and spiritual warfare that involves identifying and understanding the spiritual influences, strongholds, and dynamics affecting a particular location, region, or community. The goal is to discern the underlying spiritual forces that may hinder God's work or promote negative influences and to develop targeted prayer strategies to counter these forces.

Key Aspects of Spiritual Mapping:

- **Research and Observation**: Gathering information about the history, culture, and prevalent issues in a community. This might include studying the religious practices, patterns of sin, or significant events that could have spiritual implications.
- **Discernment of Spiritual Strongholds**: Identifying spiritual strongholds such as principalities, powers, or influences that may be affecting the people or region. This helps

believers understand the spiritual barriers that need to be addressed through prayer.

- **Targeted Prayer Strategies**: Using the insights gained through spiritual mapping to inform and direct prayers that address specific strongholds or issues, aligning them with God's will and purpose.
- Spiritual mapping involves collaborating with other believers to share insights and pray collectively for a breakthrough in the spiritual climate of the area.

Purpose of Spiritual Mapping:

- **Empowerment in Prayer**: Equips believers to pray with specificity and insight, making their intercessory efforts more strategic and effective.
- **Spiritual Breakthroughs**: Helps to identify and dismantle spiritual strongholds that may be hindering the spread of the gospel or the spiritual growth of the community.
- **Spiritual Awareness**: Fosters a deeper understanding of how the spiritual realm intersects with everyday life and influences societal dynamics.

Spiritual Mapping in Practice:

An example could be studying a city's history of violence or occult practices to understand potential spiritual strongholds. Believers might then pray against these influences, asking God for protection, healing, and the breaking of any strongholds that have taken root.

By implementing spiritual mapping, believers can engage in more focused and effective intercessory prayer, positioning themselves as instruments for God's transformative power in their communities and beyond. To do this effectively, ask the Holy Spirit for revelation and guidance. He will lead you into all truths and bring to your remembrance things that He has revealed to you. Remember, our dependence is not on what we know but on the Holy Spirit.

Biblical Foundations for Spiritual Mapping

While the term "spiritual mapping" in itself is not explicitly mentioned in the Bible, there are several examples and principles that illustrate the practice of discerning spiritual strongholds and understanding the spiritual atmosphere of a place to guide strategic action and prayer. Here are a few notable biblical examples:

Paul in Athens:

In *Acts 17:16-34*, the Apostle Paul provides an example of discerning the spiritual climate of a city. When he arrived in Athens, he observed the city was full of idols and recognised the stronghold of idolatry.

Joshua's Conquest and the Spiritual Assessment of Canaan:

Before entering the Promised Land, God instructed Joshua and the Israelite leaders to gather detailed information about the land and its inhabitants: *"Go view the land, especially Jericho."* **Joshua 2:1**

The reconnaissance mission led by Joshua's spies provided essential insight not just about the physical conditions but also about the spiritual climate and the fear the Canaanites had of Israel's God. This informed their strategy for conquest, including the spiritual acts of marching around Jericho and blowing trumpets, as described in *Joshua 6*, which had significant spiritual and symbolic implications.

The above examples show how, by spying out an area and using discernment, we can gain an insight into how the enemy keeps people in bondage. Armed with this wonderful amount of wisdom and information, we must always keep in mind that our help comes from God.

Getting to Know the Enemy

When I first came to Christ as a new believer, the Holy Spirit prompted me to study the nature of the enemy. Initially, I did not understand why this was necessary, and the very thought of delving into knowledge about the devil filled me with fear. I hesitated to embark on this journey for a long time as it seemed daunting. However, the Holy Spirit saw my fear and guided me until I became fearless.

Now, I understand that this prompting originated from a heavenly conversation. There was a moment in heaven when the sons of God came to present themselves before the Lord, and Satan also appeared among them. God asked Satan,

"Whence comest thou?" to which he responded, *"From going to and fro in the earth, and from walking up and down in it."* **Job 1:7.**

Then God said, *"Hast thou considered my servant Lance Jones?"*

This divine encounter reminds me of Satan, who actively seeks to destroy those who are devoted to God, but it is through this testing that faith is refined and spiritual authority is established.

The introduction of the enemy into my life brought significant spiritual and physical challenges, turmoil, and pain. To this day, these experiences have compelled me to seek God fervently, pray without ceasing, and develop a deep understanding of who my adversary is. As a result, I am no longer afraid or intimidated by the devil, nor am I ignorant of his schemes. I know the source of my strength and the One who empowers me.

The Importance of Knowing Our Enemy

As believers, understanding the nature of our enemy is essential. These unseen spiritual forces work strategically to undermine God's kingdom and hinder our spiritual growth.

"Lest Satan should get an advantage of us: for we are not ignorant of his devices." **2 Corinthians 2:11**

The Devil Does Not Play Fair

One of the greatest mistakes a believer can make is assuming that the devil fights with honour. He is not bound by rules of fairness, nor does he operate with any sense of mercy or restraint. Unlike God, who is just and righteous, Satan is the embodiment of deception, destruction, and cruelty. He has no compassion, no sense of remorse, and no desire for peace—his only mission is to steal, kill, and destroy.

Satan does not wait for an opportune time when you feel strong—he strikes when you are weak, weary, and vulnerable. He attacks the mind with fear, doubt, and deception. He whispers lies that cause people to question their worth, their calling, and even their salvation. He sows seeds of confusion in relationships, stirring up strife, bitterness, and division. He influences governments, media, and culture to promote immorality, rebellion, and everything that opposes God. He afflicts the body with sickness, burdens the heart with depression, and ensnares the soul with addiction and bondage.

He does not work alone—he uses his demons to go about doing his bidding, conducting his schemes of oppression and deception. These demonic forces operate in the unseen realm, influencing people, situations, and even entire nations to fulfil Satan's agenda. They plant seeds of doubt, fuel sinful desires, and seek to keep individuals trapped in cycles of fear, bondage, and destruction. Wherever there is confusion, violence, or perversion, the fingerprints of demonic activity can be found.

The devil plays dirty because he knows his time is short. He uses fear to paralyse, deception to manipulate, and temptation to ensnare. He disguises himself as an angel of light, making evil appear good and sin seem harmless. He knows how to exploit human weakness and uses every tool at his disposal—false doctrine, demonic oppression, pride, lust, greed, and even discouragement—to separate people from God. His tactics are relentless, but as believers, we are not without power. God has given us the authority to stand against the devil, to rebuke his schemes, and to walk in victory through Jesus Christ.

Though the enemy does not fight fair, he is already defeated. The blood of Jesus has stripped him of his power, and those who stand in Christ have the victory. The battle is fierce, but the outcome has already been determined—Satan's kingdom will fall, and the kingdom of God will reign forever.

The Bible also highlights the hierarchy of spiritual forces that believers face:

"For we wrestle not against flesh and blood, but against principalities, against powers, against the rulers of the darkness of this world, against spiritual wickedness in high places." **Ephesians 6:12**

Principalities and Powers

Principalities are high-ranking spiritual authorities within the demonic realm, influencing entire regions, systems, and nations.

"For by him were all things created, that are in heaven, and that are in earth, visible and invisible, whether they be thrones, or dominions, or principalities, or powers: all things were created by him, and for him." **Colossians 1:16**

The Story of the Prince of Persia and the Prince of Greece

The book of Daniel provides a vivid example of the battle involving principalities. While Daniel was fasting and praying for understanding, an angel appeared and explained the delay in delivering his response:

"But the prince of the kingdom of Persia withstood me one and twenty days: but, lo, Michael, one of the chief princes, came to help me; and I remained there with the kings of Persia." **Daniel 10:13**

This passage illustrates the significant influence that principalities have over regions. The intervention of Michael, the archangel, was necessary for the angel to break through and deliver God's message. Later, the angel mentions another impending battle:

"And now will I return to fight with the prince of Persia: and when I am gone forth, lo, the prince of Grecia shall come." **Daniel 10:20**

This demonstrates that different principalities oversee different territories and time periods, shaping the spiritual landscape according to their influence.

Powers and Their Influence

"Powers" refer to demonic authorities that exert control over certain domains, often opposing individuals' faith and spiritual growth. These forces resist God's purposes, seeking to hinder spiritual progress by promoting doubt, fear, and darkness. Through prayer and spiritual warfare, believers can break these oppressive influences and walk in the freedom that Christ has provided.

Rulers of the Darkness of This World

The rulers of the darkness of this world are spiritual entities that perpetuate sin, deception, and blindness, keeping people distant from God's truth.

"For where envying and strife is, there is confusion and every evil work." **James 3:16**

These forces promote lies, immorality, and hopelessness. However, through prayer and the declaration of God's Word, believers can expose and dismantle these works of darkness, bringing the light of Christ into spiritually oppressed areas.

Spiritual Wickedness in High Places

Spiritual wickedness in high places refers to demonic forces that corrupt the understanding of God's truth and attack believers' faith. These influences infiltrate and distort spiritual truths, often sowing confusion within the Church.

"And no marvel; for Satan himself is transformed into an angel of light." **2 Corinthians 11:14**

Praying for discernment and standing firm in Biblical truth enables believers to resist these deceptions and walk in spiritual clarity.

The Strong Man and Strongholds

Jesus described the **strong man** as a controlling spiritual force that must be bound in order to release those under his influence:

The **"strong man"** is often seen as a ruling or chief demonic spirit that exerts authority over other lesser spirits. He is believed to be the dominant force that controls or governs various forms of bondage, sin, or oppression, with other demons acting under his influence.

We need to discover who the strongman is before we can effectively bring some into absolute deliverance.

"Or else how can one enter into a strong man's house, and spoil his goods, except he first binds the strong man? and then he will spoil his house." **Matthew 12:29**

Strongholds, on the other hand, are mental, emotional, or spiritual barriers that prevent individuals from experiencing the freedom found in Christ. Recognising and breaking these strongholds through God's truth is essential for spiritual growth.

Serpents and Scorpions: Symbols of Spiritual Threats

The Bible uses serpents and scorpions as symbols of demonic threats and afflictions. Serpents represent **cunning deception**, as seen in the Garden of Eden:

"Behold, I send you forth as sheep in the midst of wolves: be ye therefore wise as serpents, and harmless as doves." **Matthew 10:16**

Scorpions symbolise **pain and torment**, reflecting spiritual attacks that test a believer's faith:

"And there came out of the smoke locusts upon the earth: and unto them was given power, as the scorpions of the earth have power." **Revelation 9:3-5**

Despite these threats, Christ has given believers authority over all the power of the enemy:

"Behold, I give unto you power to tread on serpents and scorpions, and over all the power of the enemy: and nothing shall by any means hurt you." **Luke 10:19**

The Enemy's Strategies

Understanding the enemy's tactics helps believers remain vigilant:

1. **Deception and Confusion** – Satan sows lies to lead believers astray, as seen in the Garden of Eden:
   "Yea, hath God said…?" **Genesis 3:1**
2. **Division and Strife** – The enemy aims to create discord within families and communities:
   "For where envying and strife is, there is confusion and every evil work." **James 3:16**
3. **Distraction from Spiritual Priorities** – The enemy uses worldly distractions to weaken spiritual focus. One of the greatest distractions is social media. To some, it is an addiction that has overtaken the need to watch Television, which is also a major distraction:
   "And take heed to yourselves, lest at any time your hearts be overcharged with surfeiting, and drunkenness, and **cares of this life."** **Luke 21:34**

Victory Through Christ

Understanding the enemy and his operations is crucial for reinforcing our spiritual position through **discernment, prayer, and Scripture**. This knowledge empowers believers to remain **vigilant and victorious** in their daily walk. It is important to remember that God has equipped us with everything we need for spiritual victory:

"According as his divine power hath given unto us all things that pertain unto life and godliness, through the knowledge of him that hath called us to glory and virtue." **2 Peter 1:3**

This divine assurance means that we are **well-prepared** to face any spiritual challenge. As we now shift our focus to **prayer and Intercession**—Something that a lot of believers struggle with, yet it is such a simple and effective part of our walk with God.

Prayer and Intercession

Prayer is one of the most powerful tools entrusted to believers, acting as a direct line of communication with God. It is not merely the act of speaking words; it is an expression of faith that invites divine intervention and aligns the believer's heart with God's will.

I have always said that prayer, in its simplest form, is a conversation with God—a dialogue. However, I have come to realise that many individuals are reluctant to engage in this conversation, which I find truly astonishing. For when one enters the presence of God, there is fullness of joy, and at His right hand, there are eternal pleasures. In that moment, time seems to stand still, hunger fades, and an overwhelming sense of joy fills the heart.

Intercession, a significant form of prayer, goes further by standing in the gap for others, advocating on their behalf, and seeking God's help in situations where they may be unable to pray for themselves. This chapter will delve into the nature, purpose, and profound impact of both prayer and intercession in spiritual warfare.

The Power of Prayer

The Bible is filled with examples that demonstrate the power of prayer in overcoming spiritual and physical challenges.

"The effectual fervent prayer of a righteous man availeth much." **James 5:16**

This verse underscores that prayer, when offered earnestly, carries immense power and can produce remarkable results. Prayer draws the believer closer to God, provides guidance, builds resilience, and acts as a shield against spiritual attacks. In moments of distress, prayer becomes a source of comfort and strength, enabling believers to endure and overcome trials.

"Praying always with all prayer and supplication in the Spirit, and watching thereunto with all perseverance and supplication for all saints." **Ephesians 6:18**

This passage highlights the need for continuous, Holy Spirit-led prayer to maintain spiritual vigilance.

The Power of Agreement in Prayer

One of the most profound aspects of prayer is the power of agreement.

"Again, I say unto you, that if two of you shall agree on earth as touching anything that they shall ask, it shall be done for them of my Father which is in heaven." **Matthew 18:19**

This promise emphasises that unity in prayer invites the presence and power of God, amplifying the effectiveness of intercession. I have made it a personal habit to high-five others while holding onto their hand as an act of touching and agreeing. This simple gesture reinforces the bond of faith and agreement, reminding both of us that we are united in seeking God's will and intervention.

The Role of Intercession

Intercession takes prayer beyond personal needs, focusing on the well-being of others. It embodies love, compassion, and the selfless nature of Christ, who is described as continually interceding for believers:

"Wherefore he is able also to save them to the uttermost that come unto God by him, seeing he ever liveth to make intercession for them." **Hebrews 7:25**

An intercessor stands in the spiritual gap, pleading for divine intervention on behalf of individuals, communities, or even nations. This role is exemplified by figures such as Moses, who interceded for Israel after their disobedience (*Exodus 32:11-14*), and Daniel, who prayed earnestly for the deliverance of his people (*Daniel 9:3-19*).

Why Intercession is Vital in Spiritual Warfare

Spiritual warfare is not just about resisting personal attacks; it also involves fighting for those who are oppressed or facing challenges. Intercession amplifies the collective strength of believers, creating a network of support that fortifies the body of Christ. It recognises that battles are not fought in isolation; believers are called to support one another through prayer.

"And I sought for a man among them, that should make up the hedge and stand in the gap before me for the land, that I should not destroy it: but I found none." **Ezekiel 22:30**

This verse emphasizes God's desire for individuals who will intercede on behalf of others, demonstrating that intercession can change the course of events.

Praying in Tongues: Power in the Spirit Realm

Praying in tongues or speaking in an unknown language, as enabled by the Holy Spirit, is a powerful form of prayer that transcends human understanding.

"For he that speaketh in an unknown tongue speaketh not unto men, but unto God: for no man understandeth him; howbeit in the spirit he speaketh mysteries." **1 Corinthians 14:2**

This type of prayer directly communicates with God and engages the spirit realm in ways that natural language cannot. It disrupts the enemy's plans, fortifies the believer's defences, and enables deeper spiritual alignment as the Holy Spirit intercedes beyond human comprehension.

Praying in tongues also edifies the individual:

"He that speaketh in an unknown tongue edifieth himself." **1 Corinthians 14:4**

This builds up the believer's faith, renews spiritual energy, and strengthens the connection with God.

"But ye, beloved, building up yourselves on your most holy faith, praying in the Holy Ghost." **Jude 1:20**

Keys to Effective Intercession

1. **Alignment with God's Will**: Effective intercession is guided by the Holy Spirit, ensuring that prayers align with God's purposes.

"Likewise, the Spirit also helpeth our infirmities: for we know not what we should pray for as we ought: but the Spirit itself maketh intercession for us with groanings which cannot be uttered." **Romans 8:26**

2. **Perseverance**: Intercessory prayer often requires persistence. Faith must remain strong,

even when immediate results are not visible. Jesus' parable of the persistent widow (*Luke 18:1-8*) shows that continual prayer can bring justice and breakthrough.

3. **Compassion and Empathy**: True intercession is fuelled by a heart of compassion. It involves entering into another's burden and lifting them up to God with genuine care.

"Look not every man on his own things, but every man also on the things of others." **Philippians 2:4**

1. **Faith and Authority**: Believers are given authority to pray with boldness.

"And whatsoever ye shall ask in my name, that will I do, that the Father may be glorified in the Son. If ye shall ask anything in my name, I will do it." **John 14:13-14**

The Impact of Intercession

Intercession can bring transformation, healing, and deliverance, shifting spiritual atmospheres and inviting God's presence into difficult situations. The Bible is filled with examples of communities saved, battles won, and individuals healed through intercessory prayer. Abraham's intercession for Sodom (*Genesis 18:22-33*) illustrates the influence of persistent and heartfelt prayer and reflects God's readiness to respond to the prayers of His people.

Prayer and intercession are essential elements of spiritual warfare. They fortify individual believers and create a collective shield that supports the broader community of faith. Believers are called to be watchful, prayerful, and intercessory warriors, standing firm in the power of the Holy Spirit and wielding the weapon of prayer to achieve victory and bring hope to others. The call to intercede is an invitation to partner with God, stand in the gap for those in need, and witness the transformative power of persistent prayer. Through prayer and intercession, believers align with God's heart, demonstrating love and advancing His kingdom.

Through Prayer and intercession, we can perceive who the strongman is and discover and dismantle strongholds. However, there is nothing greater than being invited by the Holy Spirit to commune with God in conversation.

Do not allow the devil to make prayer seem like a burden; push past how you feel and talk to God.

Discover and Dismantle Strongholds

A physical stronghold is a heavily fortified structure built for defence and protection. In the spiritual realm, strongholds act similarly as entrenched patterns of thinking, beliefs, or behaviours that hinder spiritual freedom and growth. Understanding and dismantling these barriers is essential for maintaining victory in spiritual warfare.

Strongholds do not form overnight; they develop through experiences, beliefs, and spiritual influences. Here is how they take root:

1. **Seeds of Deception and Misinformation:**

   Strongholds often begin with a single seed of deception or false belief planted through negative experiences or exposure to untruths. Over time, these seeds grow into pervasive ideas that challenge God's truth.

2. **Reinforcement Through Repetition:**

Repeated exposure to false beliefs, whether through thoughts, words, or external influences, strengthens these strongholds. This process deepens through negative self-talk, societal norms, or ungodly ideas.

3. **Emotional Attachment and Defensiveness:**

Strongholds often have emotional components, making them resistant to change. Fear, guilt, or past pain can anchor these barriers, making them difficult to confront and dismantle.

4. **Spiritual Influences and Demonic Oppression:**

While strongholds can develop naturally, they are also reinforced spiritually. The enemy exploits weaknesses in believers' minds to establish strongholds. *"Neither give place to the devil."* **Ephesians 4:27**

5. **Resistance to God's Truth:**

Strongholds create barriers that resist God's truth, manifesting as doubt, scepticism, or rejection of biblical teachings. This resistance makes them self-sustaining.

6. **Justification and Rationalisation:**

   Justifying destructive behaviours or thought patterns strengthens strongholds, making them harder to dismantle.

Strongholds are constructed through deception, emotional attachment, and spiritual interference. Understanding their development helps believers break free by identifying false beliefs, confronting emotional attachments, and recognising spiritual influences.

"For the weapons of our warfare are not carnal, but mighty through God to the pulling down of strongholds; casting down imaginations, and every high thing that exalteth itself against the knowledge of God, and bringing into captivity every thought to the obedience of Christ." **2 Corinthians 10:4-5**

Strategies for Breaking Strongholds

1. **Renewing the Mind**: Replace falsehoods with Scripture.
   "And be not conformed to this world: but be ye transformed by the renewing of your mind." **Romans 12:2**

2. **Persistent Prayer**: Align with God and resist the enemy.
   "Submit yourselves therefore to God. Resist the devil, and he will flee from you." **James 4:7**

3. **Confession and Support**: Share struggles for mutual support.

4. *"Iron sharpeneth iron; so a man sharpeneth the countenance of his friend."* **Proverbs 27:17**

5. **Fasting for Breakthroughs**: Intensifies reliance on God. *"Is not this the fast that I have chosen? To loose the bands of wickedness, to undo heavy burdens, and to let the oppressed go free, and that ye break every yoke?"* **Isaiah 58**

A lot of believers do not understand their true identity, and that is because they have been conformed to the patterns of this world. There are many external voices that have influenced them over the years, which have become strongholds and areas of bondage without them even knowing.

As you read this book, ask the Holy Spirit to show you if there are areas in your life that oppose the things of God and whether they have formed strongholds.

You will never be able to walk in absolute victory and authority if you have areas in your life that God does not have access to.

Walking in Spiritual Authority

The word "authority" refers to the power or right to give orders, make decisions, or enforce obedience. It can describe the legitimate control or influence that someone or something has over others. Authority is often associated with individuals in positions of leadership, such as government officials, teachers, or parents, but it can also refer to the power that comes from knowledge, expertise, or a recognised source of truth.

In a spiritual context, authority refers to the power believers have through Christ to act, speak, and make decisions in accordance with God's will, often involving the power to bind or loose spiritual forces, heal, or deliver others. Understanding the concept of authority in the Christian faith is critical for believers who are called to walk in victory and exercise their God-given rights in Christ. This chapter delves into the nature of spiritual authority, its biblical foundation, and how it empowers believers to live out their faith with boldness and confidence.

You can never have authority or power over something you are afraid of. One of the first things that a believer should know is, "Do I have authority?" The question is, how will you know?

The question that I ALWAYS ask is: "Do you have the ability to cast out demons, and do you see the manifestation of your declarations?" if the answer is yes, then they have spiritual authority; if the answer is No, I usually find that the person being asked the question, may not fully have an understanding of what it entails

An example of lacking true spiritual authority is found in **Acts 19:13-16,** where the sons of Sceva, a group of Jewish exorcists, attempted to invoke the name of Jesus to cast out evil spirits, saying,

"We adjure you by Jesus whom Paul preacheth."

However, the evil spirit responded,

"Jesus, I know, and Paul I know; but who are ye?"

and then attacked them, leaving them wounded and fleeing naked. This incident underscores that true authority comes not from using Jesus' name as a formula but from a genuine relationship with Him and being empowered by the Holy Spirit.

Walking with spiritual authority is essential for believers to operate effectively in spiritual warfare. Jesus granted His followers authority over all the power of the enemy, as recorded in Luke 10:19:

"Behold, I give unto you power to tread on serpents and scorpions, and over all the power of the enemy: and nothing shall by any means hurt you." **Luke 10:19**

This authority is not derived from human strength but from the victory Christ secured on the cross. All power and authority belong to God, who is the ultimate source of strength and dominion. In His sovereignty, He delegates this power and authority to believers, enabling them to fulfil His will on Earth and engage in spiritual warfare with confidence.

To understand this delegated power and authority, it is essential to recognise that believers have both the strength provided by God and the right to exercise it over spiritual forces. This distinction underscores that authority is not just capability but the rightful position to act.

When Jesus sent out His disciples, He imparted both His power and authority to them, enabling them to heal the sick, cast out demons, and proclaim the Kingdom of God Luke 9:1-2. This act demonstrated that God's authority could be delegated and exercised by those who believed in Him. When the disciples returned, they were filled with excitement, saying,

"Lord, even the devils are subject unto us through thy name"
Luke 10:17.

This moment highlighted their realisation of the power that had been entrusted to them and their amazement at the results.

However, Jesus responded with a teaching moment:

"Marvel not that the spirits are subject unto you; but rather rejoice, because your names are written in heaven." **Luke 10:20.**

His response indicated that the disciples were excited about something that all believers have access to, a truth that should be a consistent reality in their lives, not a cause for momentary amazement. Jesus was redirecting their focus from the act of wielding power to the deeper significance of their relationship with God and the eternal assurance that comes with it. This statement serves as a reminder that while the power to overcome the enemy is significant, the greater joy lies in the believer's connection with God and the salvation He provides.

Walking in spiritual authority requires believers to recognise their identity in Christ and act in alignment with God's Word. Ephesians 2:6 underscores this identity:

"And hath raised us up together, and made us sit together in heavenly places in Christ Jesus."

This positioning affirms that believers share in Christ's victory and authority over spiritual forces. Exercising this authority involves speaking and acting with conviction, knowing that the authority comes from Christ's finished work on the cross. James 4:7 supports this:

"Submit yourselves therefore to God. Resist the devil, and he will flee from you."

When believers resist the enemy, they do so with the confidence that comes from their rightful authority in Christ.

It is essential to pair this authority with humility and dependence on God. Without this balance, misuse or neglect of spiritual authority can lead to vulnerability. The account involving the sons of Sceva serves as a cautionary example, showing that authority must be rooted in a true relationship with Christ. Regular prayer, worship, and communion with God strengthen a believer's awareness of their authority, empowering them to walk boldly. As believers grow in their understanding of their spiritual position, they gain confidence in asserting God's power over any opposing force. Walking in spiritual authority is an ongoing journey of faith, anchored in the knowledge that Christ's victory is the foundation for every battle faced.

As believers, it is essential to understand that our true strength does not come from our own abilities or efforts. The Bible reminds us repeatedly that our reliance must be on God alone. The notion that we can achieve victory or accomplish great things solely through our own power or might is contrary to the teachings of Scripture.

"Not by might, nor by power, but by my spirit, saith the Lord of hosts." **Zechariah 4:6,**

This verse highlights a crucial truth: it is not our physical strength, resources, or influence that brings success but the power of God's Spirit. The Lord Himself is the source of our strength, guidance, and provision.

Anchored In God's Power

Relying on God fully is not just an act of faith but a conscious commitment that fortifies believers during spiritual warfare. Trusting in His strength and guidance, rather than one's own abilities, is a foundational principle for maintaining spiritual resilience.

"Trust in the LORD with all thine heart; and lean not unto thine own understanding. In all thy ways acknowledge him, and he shall direct thy paths." **Proverbs 3:5-6**

Dependence on God is strengthened through consistent prayer, study of His Word, and active reflection on His promises. This reliance ensures that believers stay connected to their divine source of power. The story of King Jehoshaphat in *2 Chronicles 20* exemplifies this truth. When faced with a vast army, he proclaimed a fast and sought the Lord's help, declaring,

"O our God, wilt thou not judge them? For we have no might against this great company that cometh against us; neither know we what to do: but our eyes are upon thee." **2 Chronicles 20:12**

God responded to their trust by granting a miraculous victory, proving that dependence on Him leads to deliverance.

True reliance on God also involves surrendering control. Accepting that God's wisdom surpasses human understanding enables believers to relinquish their anxieties and place their faith in His capable hands.

"I can do all things through Christ which strengtheneth me."
Philippians 4:13

Building a lifestyle of dependence on God includes gratitude, worship, and obedience. These elements not only draw believers closer to Him but fortify their spirit, making them resilient against spiritual attacks. Through prayer, fasting, and unwavering trust in His sovereignty, believers grow in their ability to withstand and overcome trials.

Throughout my journey as a believer, I have experienced countless moments where relying on the Holy Spirit was essential for wisdom, patience, revelation, and boldness in facing challenges. There have been times when I encountered situations that required more insight than I could provide on my own. In those moments, the Holy Spirit was my guide, offering divine wisdom that illuminated my path. One experience stands out when I had to make a decision that would impact not just me but those around me. As I prayed and sought

God, the Holy Spirit provided direction that, though unexpected, was exactly what was needed. This taught me that His wisdom is always perfect and complete, surpassing any human understanding.

Patience has become a valuable lesson in my walk of faith. I have found that waiting on the Lord allows for spiritual growth and alignment with His divine timing. During seasons when answers did not come immediately, the Holy Spirit would remind me to be still and trust in Him. I often leaned on the promise of

"Wait on the LORD: be of good courage, and he shall strengthen thine heart: wait, I say, on the LORD." **Psalm 27:14**

These moments of waiting brought a deep sense of peace and understanding, showing me that God's timing is always perfect and full of purpose.

There have been times when the Holy Spirit prompted me to step out in boldness, even when it meant facing challenges head-on. Knowing I was following God's leading always resulted in victories, breakthroughs, or blessings.

The Holy Spirit plays an indispensable role in guiding, empowering, and protecting believers.

"But ye shall receive power, after that the Holy Ghost is come upon you:" **Acts 1:8**

This divine empowerment equips believers to face spiritual adversaries with strength beyond their own.

One of the primary functions of the Holy Spirit is to provide discernment. In moments of spiritual conflict, He reveals hidden truths and exposes the enemy's strategies.

"Howbeit when he, the Spirit of truth, is come, he will guide you into all truth." **John 16:13**

This guidance is crucial for navigating spiritual challenges with wisdom and clarity. Neglecting to engage with the Holy Spirit can render Him a passive presence rather than an active force. When believers rely solely on their own understanding, they limit the Holy Spirit's transformative power and guidance. This self-reliance can lead to spiritual exhaustion, as human effort alone cannot sustain victory in spiritual battles. On the other hand, engaging the Holy Spirit through prayer and intentional reliance invites His leadership, empowering believers to walk in God's strength.

The Holy Spirit also intercedes for believers.

"Likewise the Spirit also helpeth our infirmities: for we know not what we should pray for as we ought: but the Spirit itself maketh intercession for us with groanings which cannot be uttered." **Romans 8:26**

This divine intercession provides comfort and reinforces the believer's strength during overwhelming battles. Empowerment through the Holy Spirit is evident in the way He fortifies believers for their calling. The apostles experienced this at Pentecost when they were filled with the Holy Spirit and boldly proclaimed the gospel despite fierce opposition. This same empowerment is available to believers today, granting them courage and conviction for spiritual warfare.

Living in tune with the Holy Spirit requires intentional surrender and an open heart to His leading.

"This I say then, Walk in the Spirit, and ye shall not fulfil the lust of the flesh." **Galatians 5:16**

By aligning one's life with His guidance, believers maintain a position of strength and righteousness, ensuring they remain vigilant and victorious in spiritual trials.

Strive to cultivate a strong and meaningful relationship with the Holy Spirit, who is also known as the Helper. Make Him an active part of your daily life, empowering you to live in God's strength and purpose while standing on the promises of God.

When we remain anchored in God's power, we can confidently stand on His promises, knowing He is faithful.

Standing on God's Promises

In the heat of spiritual warfare, the promises of God serve as an unwavering foundation. These promises are not just comforting words but powerful declarations of God's faithfulness and love, providing strength and assurance. Joshua 23:14 attests to this reliability: *"And, behold, this day I am going the way of all the earth: and ye know in all your hearts and in all your souls, that not one thing hath failed of all the good things which the LORD your God spake concerning you; all are come to pass unto you, and not one thing hath failed thereof."* **Joshua 23:14**

Standing on God's promises requires a deep understanding and trust in His Word. When challenges arise, reciting and meditating on scriptures like the following can strengthen you. *"Fear thou not; for I am with thee: be not dismayed; for I am thy God: I will strengthen thee; yea, I will help thee; yea, I will uphold thee with the right hand of my righteousness."* **Isaiah 41:10**

God's promises also include protection and victory in battles.

"He shall cover thee with his feathers, and under his wings shalt thou trust: his truth shall be thy shield and buckler. Thou shalt not be afraid for the terror by night; nor for the arrow that flieth by day… A thousand shall fall at thy side, and ten thousand at thy right hand; but it shall not come nigh thee." **Psalm 91:4-7**

These assurances help believers remain steadfast, knowing that God's Word never returns void *Isaiah 55:11*.

One of the most remarkable examples of holding onto God's promises is Abraham's story. God made a promise to Abraham that he would be the father of many nations, even though he and his wife Sarah were advanced in age and without children. Abraham's trust in God's promise was unwavering. After many years of waiting, and despite the impossible circumstances, God delivered on His promise, blessing Abraham and Sarah with a son, Isaac. Abraham's faith in God's promise was not in vain, and the birth of Isaac demonstrated God's faithfulness.

Similarly, I, too, experienced a promise from God that seemed impossible at the time. Through dreams and visions, God promised to bless me with my own house. I held onto this promise, even though the path to it seemed uncertain. As I waited on the Lord, trusting in His timing, the vision eventually came to pass. My own house became a reality, just as God had shown me. Just as God fulfilled His promise to Abraham, He fulfilled His promise to me, proving that when we stand firm in faith, God's promises always come to pass in His perfect timing.

Actively holding onto God's promises involves faith, prayer, patience, and affirmation. Speaking these promises aloud reaffirms trust in God and drives away doubt and fear. Such declarations shift the spiritual atmosphere and empower believers to face challenges with confidence. By embedding God's promises into daily life, believers are equipped to handle spiritual warfare with unwavering assurance.

In the next chapter, we will delve into how to remain vigilant to keep your peace; where your peace is, there also your strength will be.

"For the joy of the LORD is your strength." **Nehemiah 8:10**

Spiritual Vigilance

The word **"vigilant"** means to be **watchful, alert, and cautious**, especially to detect danger or avoid harm. It describes a state of constant awareness and readiness to respond to threats.

In a **spiritual context**, being **vigilant** means staying spiritually aware, discerning, and prepared against the enemy's schemes. This aligns with **1 Peter 5:8**:

"Be sober, be vigilant; because your adversary the devil, as a roaring lion, walketh about, seeking whom he may devour." **1 Peter 5:8**

Spiritual warfare does not end with a single victory; it is an ongoing process requiring consistent vigilance and maintenance.

"Wherefore take unto you the whole armour of God, that ye may be able to withstand in the evil day, and having done all, to stand." **Ephesians 6:13**.

This verse underscores the importance of remaining steadfast and alert, even during moments of peace. Maintaining spiritual vigilance is crucial for guarding the victories won in spiritual warfare. It is not enough to gain ground spiritually; believers must stay alert and active to preserve it.

"Praying always with all prayer and supplication in the Spirit, and watching thereunto with all perseverance and supplication for all saints." **Ephesians 6:18**.

Key Elements of Vigilance

1. **Daily Commitment to Prayer**: Constant communication with God is essential to staying spiritually prepared. *"Continue in prayer, and watch in the same with thanksgiving."* **Colossians 4:2**. Daily prayer reinforces spiritual armour, ensuring believers are always ready to face potential attacks.

2. **Studying and Meditating on Scripture**: Regular engagement with God's Word sharpens spiritual awareness. *"Thy word have I hid in mine heart, that I might not sin against thee."* **Psalm 119:11**. Consistent study ensures that believers are not caught off guard when challenges arise.

3. **Guarding Against Complacency**: Periods of peace can lead to a false sense of security. *"Be sober, be vigilant; because your adversary the devil, as a roaring lion, walketh about, seeking whom he may devour."* **1 Peter 5:8**. Maintaining spiritual

discipline even in calm times is crucial for long-term resilience.

Practices for Strengthening Spiritual Armour

- **Worship and Praise**: Regular worship invigorates the spirit and invites God's presence, creating a protective barrier. *"But thou art holy, O thou that inhabitest the praises of Israel."* **Psalm 22:3**. Worship reinforces divine protection and empowers believers.
- **Community Support**: Staying connected with other believers fosters accountability and mutual encouragement. *"Not forsaking the assembling of ourselves together, as the manner of some is; but exhorting one another: and so much the more, as ye see the day approaching."* **Hebrews 10:25**.

Maintaining Your Joy

Maintaining joy is vital in spiritual warfare, as it acts as a source of strength. The disciples were filled with joy and the Holy Ghost, a joy that transcended their circumstances and was deeply rooted in God's presence and empowerment.

"And the disciples were filled with joy, and with the Holy Ghost." **Acts 13:52**.

In His wisdom, God foresaw that His people would face persecution and trials. In anticipation of these challenges, He granted them joy, not as a fleeting emotion but as a steady and supernatural strength to persevere through difficult times. This joy was not simply a reaction to earthly circumstances but an anchor for the soul, grounded in the hope of eternal life and the promises of God.

"Rejoicing in hope; patient in tribulation; continuing instant in prayer." **Romans 12:12**.

Joy rooted in hope provides the strength to endure hardships and remain steadfast in the faith. As believers, our hope is in the resurrection of Jesus Christ, which promises victory over suffering and the assurance of eternal life.

"Blessed be the God and Father of our Lord Jesus Christ, which according to his abundant mercy hath begotten us again unto a lively hope by the resurrection of Jesus Christ from the dead." **1 Peter 1:3**.

This hope is a firm foundation, enabling believers to stand strong in the face of persecution, knowing that God's promises are sure and unshakable.

"And not only so, but we glory in tribulations also: knowing that tribulation worketh patience; and patience, experience; and experience, hope: And hope maketh not ashamed; because the love

of God is shed abroad in our hearts by the Holy Ghost which is given unto us." **Romans 5:3-5**.

The joy of the Lord is a source of strength, enabling believers to rejoice even during trials. It is a joy that brings resilience, sustaining believers through the most difficult circumstances.

"For the joy of the LORD is your strength." **Nehemiah 8:10**.

This joy fortifies the spirit, making it possible for believers to face spiritual battles with courage and unwavering faith. To keep this joy alive, believers must continually focus on God's promises and maintain a heart of gratitude. Worship, surrounding oneself with supportive believers, and reflecting on God's goodness all contribute to sustaining the joy that strengthens the believer's spirit. Engaging in worship and fellowship helps to renew the believer's mind and heart, reminding them of God's faithfulness and His power to bring victory in every circumstance.

Fellowship and Self-Examination

Spiritual vigilance also involves regular self-examination and reflection.

"Search me, O God, and know my heart: try me, and know my thoughts: And see if there be any wicked way in me, and lead me in the way everlasting." **Psalm 139:23-24**.

By seeking God's guidance and correction, believers can identify vulnerabilities and areas that require reinforcement. Fellowshipping with other believers is vital for sustaining vigilance.

"But exhort one another daily, while it is called To day; lest any of you be hardened through the deceitfulness of sin." **Hebrews 3:13**.

Engaging in fellowship and mutual encouragement helps believers stay resilient and accountable, fostering spiritual growth.

The Importance of Spiritual Covering

Spiritual covering refers to the protective and supportive role that leaders and fellow believers play in a person's spiritual life. It ensures no one fights alone and provides the prayerful support needed to withstand spiritual warfare.

"Two are better than one; because they have a good reward for their labour. For if they fall, the one will lift up his fellow: but woe to him that is alone when he falleth; for he hath not another to help him up. ... And if one prevail against him, two shall

withstand him; and a threefold cord is not quickly broken."
Ecclesiastes 4:9-12.

Having spiritual covering means fellowship with trusted believers and being under the guidance of seasoned spiritual leaders who offer wisdom, prayer, and support. This creates a fortified community where each member thrives and withstands spiritual battles.

Picking Your Battles

Engaging in every visible struggle can lead to spiritual fatigue and reduced effectiveness. Believers should seek guidance to prioritise which strongholds to address according to God's direction. Practical wisdom for battle selection includes:

- **Seek Divine Guidance**: Pause and seek the Holy Spirit's confirmation before acting to avoid unnecessary conflicts and ensure focused effort.
- **Assess Spiritual Readiness**: Ensure spiritual preparation before confronting strongholds, strengthening confidence, and reducing vulnerability.
- **Collaborate with Others**: Unified prayer with fellow believers is powerful for battles that require a collective effort. *"And if one prevail against him, two shall withstand him; and a threefold cord is not quickly broken."* **Ecclesiastes 4:12**.

Choosing battles wisely means recognising that timing and preparation are key.

"After years of understanding spiritual warfare, I choose my battles wisely, and I only go to battle when instructed by the Lord. This helps me to maintain my strength and not become fatigued."

While vigilance is essential, it is equally important to guard against exhaustion. Let us now explore how to overcome spiritual fatigue.

Overcoming Spiritual Fatigue

Recognising spiritual fatigue is essential to overcoming it. Admitting to yourself and to God that you feel spiritually worn out is the first step toward recovery. This acknowledgement is not a sign of weakness but an act of humility and trust, allowing you to confront the issue head-on. Understanding that even the most devout believers can feel drained is comforting, as it validates the experience without guilt or shame. Taking this step helps you seek God's strength and opens the door for His renewal. Reflecting on the words of **Isaiah 40:29:**

"He giveth power to the faint; and to them that have no might he increaseth strength,"

This scripture can provide reassurance that God is ready to uplift you in your weariness.

Prioritise Rest in God's Presence

Rest is more than physical sleep; it is a deliberate pause to reconnect with God. Taking time to rest in His presence helps you refocus your mind and spirit. Jesus Himself modelled the importance of rest in **Mark 6:31:** *"Come ye yourselves apart into a desert place, and rest a while."*

This invitation to step away from daily demands underscores the significance of solitude for spiritual rejuvenation. Create intentional moments of quiet where you can pray, meditate, and simply be still. Letting go of worldly distractions allows God's peace to fill you, replenishing the energy you need to continue your spiritual journey. Embracing rest as an integral part of your walk with God helps maintain your strength and readiness for the challenges ahead.

Engage in Solitude and Reflection

Setting aside moments for solitude and reflection is a powerful way to combat spiritual fatigue. In the stillness, you can meditate on God's Word and listen for His gentle voice. **Psalm 46:10 states:** *"Be still, and know that I am God,"*

reminding believers that true renewal comes from quiet moments of surrender. Use this time to step away from the noise of daily life and immerse yourself in God's promises. Whether through prayer, reading scripture, or silent contemplation, these moments invite God's presence to refresh your soul. Solitude creates space for God's peace and strength to permeate your spirit, offering a deep sense of calm and rejuvenation that can only come from Him.

Renew Your Strength Through Scripture

Scripture holds the power to uplift and rejuvenate a weary soul. Immersing yourself in God's Word provides reassurance and a renewed sense of purpose. Passages like *Isaiah 40:29-31* emphasise God's promise to renew the strength of those who trust in Him:

"But they that wait upon the Lord shall renew their strength; they shall mount up with wings as eagles; they shall run, and not be weary; and they shall walk, and not faint." **Isaiah 40:29-31**

Reading and meditating on such verses remind you that your energy does not come from your efforts alone but from God's limitless power. Make scripture reading a daily habit, allowing His words to refresh your mind and spirit continually. In doing so, you align yourself with His will and draw on the strength He provides.

Reconnect with Worship and Prayer

Worship and prayer are vital for shifting your focus from your limitations to God's greatness. Even when spiritual fatigue makes it challenging, engaging in worship renews your spirit by reminding you of God's majesty and faithfulness. Prayer allows you to express your burdens and draw closer to the Holy Spirit. Singing hymns, speaking gratitude, or even sitting in silent reverence are all forms of worship that invite God's presence. As *Philippians 4:13* affirms,

"I can do all things through Christ which strengtheneth me,"
Philippians 4:13

trusting in this truth during worship helps you receive divine strength. Regular, heartfelt worship and honest prayer refresh your soul and deepen your connection with God, paving the way for spiritual renewal.

Seek Renewal Through Service

Renewal can often be found in serving others. When you turn your focus outward and help those in need, you tap into the joy and fulfilment that come from being God's instrument of love. Serving others shifts your perspective from your challenges to the blessings you can share. This act of giving revitalises your spirit and provides a fresh reminder of your purpose within God's kingdom. Even simple acts of kindness can reignite your passion for your faith and encourage a positive outlook. Through service, you become a conduit for God's grace, allowing Him to work through you while simultaneously strengthening your own spirit. The joy that comes from serving others acts as a powerful antidote to spiritual fatigue, filling your heart with divine purpose and energy.

We cannot always be strong, but in our moments of weakness and fatigue, let us run to the One who called us so He can prepare us for what lies ahead.

Preparing for Future Battles

Preparation for future spiritual battles is an essential part of maintaining spiritual strength and resilience. Victories in spiritual warfare are significant, but without an ongoing commitment to readiness, believers may find themselves unprepared for future challenges. Maintaining a posture of alertness ensures that believers are not only celebrating past triumphs but are also fully equipped for what lies ahead. *Ephesians 6:13* underscores that preparation is not passive but requires active and continuous engagement:

"Wherefore take unto you the whole armour of God, that ye may be able to withstand in the evil day, and having done all, to stand." **Ephesians 6:13**

Central to this preparation is a consistent relationship with God's Word. Immersing oneself in Scripture serves as both a shield and a source of enlightenment, guiding believers through the complexities of life and enabling them to identify and address areas of spiritual vulnerability. The act of regularly studying and meditating on the Word equips believers with divine insight, guiding them through the complexities of life and enabling them to identify and address areas of spiritual vulnerability. The story of David exemplifies this principle; when he confronted Goliath, his strength was not solely drawn from the sling and stones but from a heart fortified by unwavering trust in God, cultivated through years of faithful preparation.

Prayer is another cornerstone of spiritual readiness, acting as a direct line to God and a source of continuous empowerment. A robust prayer life fosters spiritual alertness, enhancing the believer's sensitivity to divine guidance and protection. This state of vigilance helps ensure they remain anchored in God's promises, ready to respond to whatever challenges may arise.

Preparation also means drawing wisdom from past experiences. Reflecting on previous battles—whether moments of triumph or times of trial, can offer invaluable lessons. These reflections strengthen the believer's faith and sharpen their spiritual discernment, making them better equipped for future encounters. Reflecting on past experiences deepens the believer's understanding of God's faithfulness and their role in standing firm through His strength.

Preparation for future spiritual battles is a continual process that shapes the believer's spiritual maturity. Engaging with Scripture, fostering an active prayer life, and learning from past experiences create a foundation that withstands the storms of adversity. By embracing these practices, believers are better positioned to stand resiliently, confident that their readiness is rooted in the unchanging power of God. Maintaining this vigilant approach ensures that, having done all, they will indeed stand.

Strengthening Faith

Resilience is the ability to recover quickly from difficulties, adapt to challenges, and remain strong in the face of adversity. It involves not only the ability to withstand hardship but also the capacity to grow stronger through trials and challenges. In a spiritual context, resilience is foundational for any believer who desires to walk steadfastly with God, especially when confronted with spiritual attacks or life's hardships. The Bible makes it clear that we are engaged in a spiritual war against an enemy who seeks to destroy us. **John 10:10** reminds us:

"The thief cometh not, but for to steal, and to kill, and to destroy: I am come that they might have life, and that they might have it more abundantly." **John 10:10**

As followers of Christ, we must be prepared to stand firm against the attacks of the enemy, knowing that our strength comes not from ourselves but from God.

Trials as a Refining Process

James 1:2-4 encourages believers in this regard:

"My brethren, count it all joy when ye fall into divers temptations; Knowing this, that the trying of your faith worketh patience. But let patience have her perfect work, that ye may be perfect and entire, wanting nothing." **James 1:2-4**

This passage reminds us that trials are not meant to break us but to refine us, making us spiritually mature and complete. Through patience, perseverance, and trust in God's plan, we become stronger and better equipped for the battles that lie ahead. Adversity, therefore, should be seen as a tool for spiritual growth rather than a setback.

Anchoring in Faith

To build resilience, believers must anchor themselves deeply in faith. Faith is more than a passive belief; it is an active, unwavering trust in God, even when circumstances seem overwhelming or discouraging. **Hebrews 11:1** defines faith as:

"Now faith is the substance of things hoped for, the evidence of things not seen." **Hebrews 11:1**

This verse teaches that faith is not about seeing immediate results or understanding every situation; rather, it is about trusting in God's promises and His divine timing, even when we cannot yet perceive His work. Trusting in God's unseen work strengthens spiritual resolve and builds a foundation that can withstand any storm. True resilience, therefore, arises from a faith that looks beyond the visible, choosing to believe in God's faithfulness and goodness no matter the circumstances.

Standing Firm in Spiritual Warfare

As believers, we are in a constant battle against the enemy, who seeks to weaken our faith and draw us away from God.

This spiritual war requires believers to remain vigilant, clothed in the full armour of God, and steadfast in prayer. The enemy will attempt to instil fear, doubt, and discouragement, but those who stand firm in their faith will overcome through Christ. 2 Corinthians 10:4 further reassures us:

"For the weapons of our warfare are not carnal, but mighty through God to the pulling down of strong holds; " **2 Corinthians 10:4**

Our strength and victory do not come from our own power but through God's divine authority and might.

Daily Meditation on God's Promises

Repetition is key when it comes to strengthening faith. Meditating daily on the promises found in Scripture fortifies the heart and mind, creating a wellspring of faith that can be drawn upon during times of hardship. **Psalm 119:11** reminds us of the power of hiding God's Word in our hearts:

"Thy word have I hid in mine heart, that I might not sin against thee." **Psalm 119:11**

When we continuously focus on God's promises, it builds a reservoir of spiritual strength, helping us face challenges with courage and hope. It is not just about memorising verses but allowing those promises to become ingrained in our hearts, serving as reminders that God is faithful.

Cultivating a Prayerful Life

A consistent prayer life is vital for building resilience. Prayer is the channel through which believers maintain communication with God, allowing them to receive peace, guidance, and strength. **Philippians 4:7** speaks of the power of prayer, stating:

"And the peace of God, which passeth all understanding, shall keep your hearts and minds through Christ Jesus." **Philippians 4:7**

When spiritual battles arise, prayer enables us to lay our burdens before God, trusting that He will give us the peace we need to endure. This peace, which surpasses human understanding, acts as a safeguard for our hearts and minds, ensuring that we do not become overwhelmed by fear or anxiety.

Practising Gratitude

Gratitude has a profound impact on building resilience. When believers focus on God's faithfulness and express thanks, even in small victories, it shifts their perspective. This practice boosts spiritual strength, reinforcing trust in God's perfect plan. **1 Thessalonians 5:18** encourages believers to give thanks in all circumstances:

"In every thing give thanks: for this is the will of God in Christ Jesus concerning you." **1 Thessalonians 5:18**

Even in times of trial, recognising God's presence and thanking Him for His continual faithfulness helps to build a resilient mindset. It teaches us to acknowledge the goodness of God, no matter the situation and helps us grow in patience, joy, and peace.

Resilience is not built overnight; it is the product of consistent, faith-filled actions. Each challenge overcome, each prayer answered, and each trial endured becomes a testament to God's power and an opportunity for growth. Even when faced with difficulty, these moments of perseverance shape believers into spiritually mature warriors who can stand firm, knowing that God is with them.

As we build resilience, we are not simply surviving but thriving in the midst of spiritual warfare, growing closer to God, and becoming more confident in His ability to equip us for every battle that comes our way. Through faith, prayer, and unwavering trust in God's promises, we can emerge victorious, standing strong against the enemy's schemes and walking boldly in the abundant life Christ has given us.

In Times of Spiritual Drought

Spiritual droughts, or periods when God seems silent, can test the faith and patience of believers. These moments are often marked by a sense of distance from God, even when prayers and spiritual practices are maintained. Yet, these times can be transformative, shaping deeper trust and reliance on God's promises. *Psalm 42:1-2* captures this longing: *"As the hart panteth after the water brooks, so panteth my soul after thee, O God. My soul thirsteth for God, for the living God."* **Psalm 42:1-2**

The four Strategies for Persevering During Droughts:

1. ***Hold Fast to the Word:***
   Isaiah 55:11 reassures believers that God's Word *"shall not return unto me void, but it shall accomplish that which I please."* **Isaiah 55:11**

Continuously studying Scripture provides sustenance even when feelings falter. When the heart feels dry, God's Word serves as a wellspring of life that never runs dry, offering direction and comfort in times of spiritual barrenness.

2. ***Maintain Worship and Praise:***Choosing to worship when it feels hardest is an act of faith that can break through spiritual dryness.

   "Although the fig tree shall not blossom… Yet I will rejoice in the Lord, I will joy in the God of my salvation." **Habakkuk 3:17-18**

   Even when circumstances seem unfruitful, making the choice to rejoice in God's sovereignty breaks through the dryness of the soul. True worship goes beyond feelings and circumstances, declaring God's greatness regardless of external situations.

3. ***Seek Fellowship and Encouragement:*** Engaging with fellow believers offers mutual support.

   "And let us consider one another to provoke unto love and to good works: Not forsaking the assembling of ourselves together." **Hebrews 10:24-25**

   In times of drought, the fellowship of other believers is a vital source of strength. Encouragement from others helps sustain the weary soul, reminding them that they are not alone in their spiritual journey.

4. ***Remember Past Faithfulness:*** Recalling how God has moved in past situations can reignite hope!

"I will remember the works of the Lord: surely I will remember thy wonders of old. I will meditate also of all thy work, and talk of thy doings." **Psalm 77:11-12**

Reflecting on God's faithfulness in previous seasons of life strengthens trust, even when the present feels uncertain. This act of remembrance helps believers recognise that God, who has been faithful in the past, will continue to be faithful in the future.

Spiritual droughts, though challenging, teach believers to rely on faith rather than feelings. They become opportunities for spiritual endurance, strengthening the believer's relationship with God and preparing them for future battles with greater resilience and trust. In times of drought, the choice to stand firm on God's Word, worship with a joyful heart, seek support from fellow believers, and remember past victories ensures that the believer emerges stronger and more rooted in faith.

Nurturing Spiritual Growth

Spiritual growth is essential for believers to thrive in their faith and remain equipped for spiritual warfare. This growth is a continuous journey that involves nurturing one's relationship with God and cultivating qualities that reflect Christ.

"But grow in grace, and in the knowledge of our Lord and Saviour Jesus Christ." **2 Peter 3:18**

Ways to Nurture Spiritual Growth:

1. Engage in Consistent Bible Study

Regular study of Scripture provides the wisdom and insight necessary for personal growth. *Psalm 1:2-3* emphasises,

"But his delight is in the law of the Lord; and in his law doth he meditate day and night. And he shall be like a tree planted by the rivers of water." **Psalm 1:2-3**

Meditating on God's Word consistently nourishes the soul and enables believers to bear fruit in all seasons of life. Bible study is foundational to spiritual growth, providing a firm grounding in God's truth.

2. Apply God's Word Practically

Growth is not only about knowledge but also about application.

"But be ye doers of the word, and not hearers only, deceiving your own selves." **James 1:22**

It is essential to put into practice what is learned from Scripture. As believers apply God's Word in everyday situations, they mature in their faith, and their lives reflect the transformative power of the gospel.

3. Maintain a Prayerful Attitude

Keeping an open line of communication with God ensures that believers stay guided and receptive to His will.

"Pray without ceasing." **1 Thessalonians 5:17**

A consistent prayer life strengthens the believer's connection with God, providing clarity, peace, and the power to face spiritual battles. Prayer also fosters humility and dependence on God, allowing His guidance to shape decisions and actions.

4. Seek Mentorship and Fellowship

Learning from mature Christians and participating in fellowship strengthens spiritual growth and accountability. *Proverbs 27:17* states,

"Iron sharpeneth iron; so a man sharpeneth the countenance of his friend." **Proverbs 27:17**

Engaging in relationships with other believers encourages mutual growth and strengthens spiritual resolve. Fellowship provides opportunities for support, accountability, and the sharing of wisdom, helping believers grow in unity and strength.

Spiritual growth involves moments of reflection, commitment to deeper prayer, and active pursuit of a life that mirrors Christ's teachings. This continuous effort builds believers into spiritually strong, equipped individuals capable of facing challenges with grace and wisdom. By nurturing a consistent relationship with God through Bible study, prayer, and fellowship, believers will grow in grace and knowledge, becoming more like Christ and more equipped to handle spiritual warfare.

Staying Rooted and Grounded

Staying rooted and grounded in faith is essential for every believer to navigate life's trials with strength and grace. Life is full of challenges that can test our commitment to God, making it even more important to develop a solid foundation. *Colossians 2:6-7* instructs,

"As ye have therefore received Christ Jesus the Lord, so walk ye in him: Rooted and built up in him, and stablished in the faith, as ye have been taught, abounding therein with thanksgiving." **Colossians 2:6-7**

Just as trees with deep roots can withstand fierce storms, believers with a firm spiritual foundation can endure trials without being uprooted.

Being rooted and grounded means consistently building a relationship with God that anchors us firmly in His truth. It involves developing spiritual habits that help us remain unwavering despite the distractions and external influences that vie for our attention. We must be deliberate about nurturing our connection with God and ensuring that nothing gets in the way of our devotion. This requires a conscious effort to guard our relationship with God and prioritise it above all else.

Staying consistent in our walk with God means setting aside intentional time each day to seek Him, meditate on His Word, and remain in prayer. It is about cultivating a mindset where our faith becomes an integral part of who we are, not just something we turn to in times of need. In a world full of noise and competing priorities, it is easy to become distracted or let other things take precedence. However, we are called to work out our salvation with fear and trembling, as *Philippians 2:12* reminds us. This underscores the seriousness of maintaining a steadfast relationship with God.

"Wherefore, my beloved, as ye have always obeyed, not as in my presence only, but now much more in my absence, work out your own salvation with fear and trembling." **Philippians 2:12**

Guarding our relationship with God involves being vigilant and discerning about what we allow to influence our hearts and minds.

External voices, societal pressures, and worldly desires can all act as hindrances if we are not careful. By focusing on God's truth and seeking His guidance in every decision, we strengthen our spiritual foundation and ensure that our devotion remains pure and undivided.

Despite these practices, there are believers who have placed their leaders on pedestals, almost making them god-like figures. If the leader falls from grace, those who have fixed their eyes on them instead of Christ can find their faith shaken. Just as Peter sank when he took his eyes off Jesus amidst the storm *Matthew 14:30*, so too do believers risk spiritual downfall when their devotion shifts from God to men.

Regardless of their spiritual strength, leaders are human and susceptible to failure. God alone is infallible, and *Hebrews 12:2* urges us to fix our eyes on Jesus, the author and finisher of our faith.

"Looking unto Jesus the author and finisher of our faith; who for the joy that was set before him endured the cross, despising the shame, and is set down at the right hand of the throne of God." **Hebrews 12:2**

From experience, I have witnessed Christians who began their journey strong in the Lord, only to face an offence that caused them to reject the church—a decision that led them to reject Christ. It is a sobering reminder that bitterness and disillusionment can erode faith. Scripture warns us in *Hebrews 3:12*,

"Take heed, brethren, lest there be in any of you an evil heart of unbelief, in departing from the living God." **Hebrews 3:12**

To stay rooted and grounded, we must be vigilant and guard our hearts. This means striving for consistency in our faith, resisting distractions, and ensuring our commitment to God is unwavering. Let us commit to these practices that reinforce our faith and keep Christ at the centre, ensuring that when trials come, we remain steadfast and unwavering in Him.

Now that we have a better understanding of what it means to be rooted and grounded in God, the following three chapters align with spiritual warfare by emphasising the practices and perspectives that equip believers to stand firm against spiritual opposition and challenges:

Together, these chapters guide believers to develop the spiritual discipline and mindset necessary for enduring and overcoming the challenges of spiritual warfare. They focus on equipping individuals to ground themselves in faith, follow Jesus' example, and walk in victory through reliance on God and adherence to His Word.

Focusing on Eternal Truths

Focusing on eternal truths means prioritising and grounding your life in the timeless and unchanging principles found in God's Word and divine teachings. These truths transcend temporary, worldly concerns and remain steadfast regardless of changing circumstances or cultural shifts. When believers focus on eternal truths, they align their thoughts, actions, and decisions with values that reflect God's character, such as love, faith, righteousness, and hope.

Keeping an eternal perspective is vital for maintaining spiritual strength and purpose. Life's temporary challenges and distractions can easily shift a believer's focus, but centring thoughts on eternal truths provides clarity and hope. *2 Corinthians 4:17-18* reminds believers:

"For our light affliction, which is but for a moment, worketh for us a far more exceeding and eternal weight of glory; While we look not at the things which are seen, but at the things which are not seen: for the things which are seen are temporal; but the things which are not seen are eternal." **2 Corinthians 4:17-18**

Practices for Maintaining an Eternal Focus:

5. *Meditating on Heaven's Promises*: Reflecting on scriptures that speak of eternal life, such as *John 14:2-3*, helps to remind believers of their future hope and the joy that awaits.

6. *"In my Father's house are many mansions... I go to prepare a place for you."* **John 14:2-3**

7. *Serving with Purpose*: Remembering that each act of service done in love is seen by God and helps believers stay motivated.

   "And let us not be weary in well doing: for in due season we shall reap, if we faint not." **Galatians 6:9**

8. *Keeping Hope Alive*: Clinging to the hope of God's promises sustains faith in difficult seasons.

   "For we are saved by hope: but hope that is seen is not hope... But if we hope for that we see not, then do we with patience wait for it." **Romans 8:24-25**

Focusing on eternal truths shifts the mindset from immediate concerns to the greater, divine plan. This perspective helps believers maintain a sense of purpose and direction, even amid life's uncertainties and challenges. Eternal truths remind us that our ultimate goal is not rooted in the temporary achievements or trials of this world but in our relationship with God and the hope of eternity with Him.

This eternal focus cultivates peace and strengthens perseverance, allowing believers to navigate life's challenges with a heart anchored in eternal joy and purpose.

Jesus Lived in the Spirit

One of the greatest mysteries of the Christian faith is the truth that Jesus Christ was both fully man and fully God. He was not merely a divine being who appeared in human form, nor was He just an extraordinary man chosen by God—He was the Word made flesh. **John 1:14** declares:

"And the Word was made flesh, and dwelt among us, (and we beheld his glory, the glory as of the only begotten of the Father,) full of grace and truth."

Jesus' humanity meant that He experienced hunger, thirst, weariness, and even temptation. He felt emotions such as joy, sorrow, and compassion. Yet, His divinity meant that He was sinless, had authority over nature, demons, and sickness, and had power over death itself. This dual nature was essential for His mission—to be the perfect mediator between God and man, the sinless sacrifice who could atone for the sins of the world.

The Bible confirms Jesus' humanity in **Hebrews 4:15**:

"For we have not an high priest which cannot be touched with the feeling of our infirmities; but was in all points tempted like as we are, yet without sin."

Though He faced the full reality of human limitations, Jesus never sinned. He overcame every trial, not by relying on His divine nature alone but by living in perfect dependence on the Holy Spirit.

Walking in the Spirit

Jesus did not operate in His own strength but lived in total submission to the will of the Father, walking in the power of the Holy Spirit. From the very beginning of His ministry, the Holy Spirit played a crucial role. When Jesus was baptised, **Luke 3:22** records:

"And the Holy Ghost descended in a bodily shape like a dove upon him, and a voice came from heaven, which said, Thou art my beloved Son; in thee I am well pleased."

Immediately after His baptism, **Luke 4:1** states:

"And Jesus being full of the Holy Ghost returned from Jordan, and was led by the Spirit into the wilderness."

His time in the wilderness, where He fasted for forty days and overcame Satan's temptations, demonstrated how He lived in the Spirit. He did not rely on human strength or logic to resist the devil but wielded the power of the Word of God, declaring, *"It is written…"* (Matthew 4:4, 7, 10).

Jesus' entire ministry was carried out in the power of the Holy Spirit. **Luke 4:14** declares:

"And Jesus returned in the power of the Spirit into Galilee: and there went out a fame of him through all the region round about."

Everything Jesus did—preaching, healing, casting out demons, performing miracles, was accomplished through the anointing of the Holy Spirit. **Acts 10:38** testifies:

"How God anointed Jesus of Nazareth with the Holy Ghost and with power: who went about doing good, and healing all that were oppressed of the devil; for God was with him."

This dependence on the Spirit was not because Jesus lacked power as God but because He chose to humble Himself and function as a man filled with the Holy Spirit. In doing so, He became the perfect example for all believers to follow.

Living in Perfect Obedience

Jesus lived in complete submission to the Father. He never acted on His own will but always sought to do the Father's will. **John 5:19** reveals:

"Then answered Jesus and said unto them, Verily, verily, I say unto you, The Son can do nothing of himself, but what he seeth the Father do: for what things soever he doeth, these also doeth the Son likewise."

His obedience was not reluctant but joyful, rooted in love and trust. Even when facing the agony of the cross, Jesus submitted to the Father's plan, praying in **Luke 22:42**:

"Saying, Father, if thou be willing, remove this cup from me: nevertheless not my will, but thine, be done."

Jesus' perfect obedience and reliance on the Holy Spirit set the standard for how believers should live. Just as He walked in the Spirit, we too are called to be led by the Spirit, to surrender our will to God, and to operate in His power rather than our own strength.

The Example for Believers

Jesus' life demonstrates that true spiritual living is not about personal effort but about dependency on the Holy Spirit. **Romans 8:14** says:

"For as many as are led by the Spirit of God, they are the sons of God."

Just as Jesus was led by the Spirit in everything He did, we, too, must walk in the Spirit daily. **Galatians 5:16** instructs:

"This I say then, Walk in the Spirit, and ye shall not fulfil the lust of the flesh."

Jesus has made it possible for us to live the same way He did. Through His death and resurrection, He not only provided salvation but also sent the Holy Spirit to dwell within us. **John 14:16-17** declares:

"And I will pray the Father, and he shall give you another Comforter, that he may abide with you for ever; Even the Spirit of truth; whom the world cannot receive, because it seeth him not, neither knoweth him: but ye know him; for he dwelleth with you, and shall be in you."

Jesus, though fully God, chose to live as a man completely dependent on the Holy Spirit, setting the perfect example for us to follow. He walked in obedience, lived in the power of the Spirit, and fulfilled the Father's will in everything He did. As believers, we are called to follow in His footsteps, allowing the Holy Spirit to guide, strengthen, and empower us for every good work.

When we walk as Jesus did—led by the Spirit, obedient to the Father, and relying on God's power rather than our own—we can live victorious, fulfilling lives that reflect His glory. **As He lived in the Spirit, so must we.**

Walking In the Spirit

There is a misconception that being "heavenly-minded" makes one "of no earthly use." This notion is often used to downplay or dismiss the importance of spiritual truths and spiritual living. The idea is that focusing on spiritual matters could somehow disconnect someone from the real, tangible needs of the world around them. But in reality, this could not be further from the truth. In fact, being heavenly-minded is precisely what enables believers to have a profound, transformative impact on the world.

Jesus Christ Himself is the perfect example of being heavenly-minded and yet profoundly impactful in the world. He prioritised His relationship with the Father and lived with a deep sense of His eternal purpose. However, He was never disconnected from the needs of the people around Him. His life and ministry were marked by radical love, service, and transformation—things that happened because He was deeply connected to heavenly realities, not in spite of them.

Spiritual Truths and Real-World Change

When people use the phrase "heavenly minded but of no earthly use," it often seems like an excuse to dismiss the application of spiritual principles in daily life. But Jesus demonstrated that living in alignment with God's will, grounded in spiritual truths, enables us to bring about lasting change in the earthly realm. It was His heavenly mindset that empowered Him to heal the sick, feed the hungry, and bring about redemption. His heavenly perspective gave Him the power to change lives on earth.

The Bible teaches that spiritual truths are not meant to be compartmentalised or separated from our daily lives. In fact, the application of spiritual truths leads to real-world change. **Matthew 6:33** instructs,

"But seek ye first the kingdom of God, and his righteousness; and all these things shall be added unto you."

Our focus on God and His kingdom should not hinder our earthly responsibilities; rather, it should enhance and direct how we live. It is when we prioritise spiritual things that we are best equipped to make a positive impact in the world.

The world often dismisses the spiritual, but it is clear that to see true, lasting change—whether in our own lives or in the lives of others—we need to live by the power of the Holy Spirit, grounded in spiritual truths. Without a heavenly perspective, we miss the full potential of what God can do through us on earth.

Aligning Our Lives with Spiritual Truths

Many people expect spiritual results without applying spiritual principles. But the Bible makes it clear that there is a connection between the way we live spiritually and the outcomes we experience in the world. It is not enough to simply hope for miracles without aligning our hearts and actions with God's will. As **James 2:17** teaches,

"Even so faith, if it hath not works, is dead, being alone."

There is a direct relationship between spiritual living and real-world results. Walking in the Spirit involves living under the guidance and influence of the Holy Spirit, allowing Him to direct our thoughts, actions, and decisions according to God's will. This way of life is marked by embodying the fruits of the Spirit, which include love, joy, peace, patience, kindness, goodness, faithfulness, gentleness, and self-control. As *Galatians 5:22-23* outlines,

"But the fruit of the Spirit is love, joy, peace, longsuffering, gentleness, goodness, faith, meekness, temperance: against such there is no law."

Seven Pillars for Walking in the Spirit

To walk in the Spirit, we must follow the example of Jesus, who showed us how to live a life that is both heavenly-minded and impactful on earth. His life demonstrates the seven essential pillars for walking in the Spirit:

1.   Constant Prayer and Communion with God:

Constant communication with God is key to walking in the Spirit. Jesus exemplified a life of constant prayer and communion with God.

"And in the morning, rising up a great while before day, he went out, and departed into a solitary place, and there prayed." Mark 1:35

2.   Obedience to God's Will:

Jesus was completely obedient to God's will, even when it led to great personal sacrifice. *"For I came down from heaven, not to do mine own will, but the will of him that sent me." John 6:38*

3.   Commitment to Scripture:

Jesus lived by God's Word. In moments of temptation, He responded with Scripture.

"It is written, Man shall not live by bread alone, but by every word that proceedeth out of the mouth of God." Matthew 4:4

4. A Pursuit of Holiness:

Jesus lived a sinless life, modelling perfect holiness. *Hebrews 4:15* assures,

"For we have not an high priest which cannot be touched with the feeling of our infirmities; but was in all points tempted like as we are, yet without sin." Hebrews 4:15.

5. Compassion, Love, and Service:

Jesus was marked by compassion, love, and service to others. *Matthew 20:28* records,

"Even as the Son of man came not to be ministered unto, but to minister, and to give his life a ransom for many." Matthew 20:28.

6. Humility and Servanthood:

Jesus modelled humility and servanthood, as shown in *Philippians 2:7-8:*

"But made himself of no reputation, and took upon him the form of a servant, and was made in the likeness of men: And being found in fashion as a man, he humbled himself, and became obedient unto death, even the death of the cross."

7. Dependence on the Holy Spirit:

Jesus depended on the Holy Spirit for guidance and power. *Luke 4:1* describes,

"And Jesus being full of the Holy Ghost returned from Jordan, and was led by the Spirit into the wilderness." Luke 4:1.

The Connection Between Heavenly Focus and Earthly Impact

By walking in the Spirit, believers are equipped to grow spiritually, resist temptation, and navigate life's challenges with strength and grace. Living a life empowered by the Holy Spirit brings not only personal transformation but also enables us to reflect Christ to the world. As *Ephesians 5:18-19* encourages,

"And be not drunk with wine, wherein is excess; but be filled with the Spirit; Speaking to yourselves in psalms and hymns and spiritual songs, singing and making melody in your heart to the Lord."

In conclusion, being heavenly-minded is absolutely essential. It is through our heavenly-minded focus that we become effective instruments of change in the world. When we walk in the Spirit, we do not become irrelevant or disconnected from the world; rather, we become the very vessels through which God's will is done on earth. As *2 Corinthians 5:20* reminds us, *"Now then we are ambassadors for Christ..."*

Let us live in the power of the Holy Spirit, guided by God's Word and empowered to bring about His kingdom on earth.

Prayer & Declaration

Prayer 1: Empowerment by the Holy Spirit

Father, I call upon You to hear my cry in the name of Jesus. I ask for Your Holy Spirit to fill me and empower me with strength and boldness. As *Acts 1:8* declares,

"But ye shall receive power, after that the Holy Ghost is come upon you." **Acts 1:8**

Lord, let Your Spirit guide me, infuse me with courage, and enable me to walk in the fullness of Your will. Strengthen my heart and mind so that I may serve You faithfully and stand firm in every situation. In the mighty name of Jesus, I pray. Amen.

Declaration 1: Empowerment by the Holy Spirit

I declare that the Holy Spirit empowers me; I walk in strength and boldness, ready to fulfil God's purpose in my life. No fear or uncertainty can deter me, for His Spirit within me is greater than any challenge I may face. I am equipped with the divine power to overcome obstacles, speak truth, and bring light into the darkest places. I am a vessel of God's strength, moving forward with unwavering faith and determination.

Prayer 2: Receiving the Gift of Discernment

Father, I call upon You to hear my cry in the name of Jesus. Your Word says in *James 1:5*,

"If any of you lack wisdom, let him ask of God, that giveth to all men liberally, and upbraideth not; and it shall be given him."

Lord, I ask for the gift of discernment—the ability to see clearly and understand the spiritual forces at work. Grant me wisdom to distinguish between truth and deception and to navigate my path with divine insight. May Your Spirit teach me to respond with righteousness and grace. In Jesus' name, I pray. Amen.

Declaration 2: Receiving the Gift of Discernment

I declare that I will receive the gift of discernment; I am equipped with divine wisdom and insight to see and act according to God's truth. My mind is sharp, and my spirit is attuned to the voice of the Holy Spirit, which enables me to recognise what is hidden and discern the righteous path. I am vigilant, alert, and protected from deception. With God's discernment, I make decisions that align with His perfect will, bringing clarity and peace to my journey.

Prayer 3: Cancelling Demonic Forces

Father, I call upon You to hear my cry in the name of Jesus. Your Word in *Luke 10:19* assures me, *"Behold, I give unto you power to tread on serpents and scorpions, and over all the power of the enemy: and nothing shall by any means hurt you."* **Luke 10:19**

I stand on this promise and command every demonic force seeking to disrupt my life to be cast out in Jesus' name. By the blood of Jesus and the authority of His name, I cancel and nullify every evil plan and declare victory over darkness. Let Your light surround me, and Your peace fill my heart. In Jesus' victorious name, I pray. Amen.

Declaration 3: Cancelling Demonic Forces
I declare that I am victorious through the blood and name of Jesus; every force of darkness is defeated, and I walk in His divine protection and peace. I am surrounded by the shield of His presence, and no evil can prevail against me. I stand firm in the victory of Christ, confident that His power is greater than any adversary. I move forward with the assurance that I am covered, guided, and strengthened by the Lord. My life is a testament to His triumph, and I live each day with boldness and peace, knowing that I am secure in His unfailing protection.

About The Author

Lance G. Jones has long harboured a dream of writing, often saying that one day he would make the time to bring his stories to life. I remember sitting with him during those early moments, watching as he prepared to write his first book, beginning with the table of contents—a foundation from which he believed the rest would flow naturally.

Now, with multiple books to his name, Lance has become an enthusiastic and dedicated author. His passion for writing shines most brightly in his children's books, where his keen sense of humour and vivid, imaginative storytelling create memorable experiences for young readers.

Among his works, Lance's Christian novel *She Went Looking for Love* garnered attention from readers worldwide, marking his debut as a published author and establishing his presence in the literary world. Additionally, he is gaining recognition with *The World of Taye Tari* series, inspired by his grandson, and is already boasting several instalments, with more on the horizon.

Given the impact Lance is making, I have no doubt we will be hearing much more from this talented author in the years ahead.

—Stephen Jones